Sunday Poems

Raph Koster

ALTERED
TUNING
PRESS

Published by Altered Tuning Press
12463 Rancho Bernardo Rd., #556
San Diego, CA 92128

ISBN-13: 978-0-9967937-0-4
ISBN-10: 0-9967937-0-4

Sunday Poems

Sunday Poems

Contents

Foreword..v
    The Sunday Poem (original introduction) vii

Why It Is Hard...1
Pistachio...2
Candy 3
Suomi 4
    Geese seen from Kaivopuisto, Helsinki *4*
After Serious Sunburn 5
The Road to Whimsy..6
Slide...7
Science Homework 8
Sometimes a Duck is Just a Duck..9
The Piano Teacher's House..10
Davey Flower Becomes a Pterodactyl....................................11
Sierras From Above 12
Clouds from Above 13
Descending to the Airport at Night 14
    San Diego from Presidio Park.. *15*
If Trees Did Not Stop Growing 16

Driving to Tainan 17
Lions in Vegas 18
A Cherufe Tale 19
Boston Photographs 20
All Stories Are Like This 21
    A church in Boston *21*
Building the Globe 23
Dead Media 24
Candy II 25
The Spencer Wheelhouse 26
Change of Dreams 27
Maid Marian 28
Amelia on Nikumaroro 29
Why Wulfric Lived to 90 30
Reactions to the Awful News 31
    I. The Preacher 31
    II. Mother Martin 32
    III. The Shopkeeper 33
    A farm in snow, Jefferson, Maryland *33*
    IV. The Teacher 33
    V. The Boy 35
    VI. Mrs. Shay 36
    VII. Old Crow 37
    VIII. The Fellow with the Suit 38
    IX. Jenny 39
    X. 40
    Storeroom barrels, Old Sturbridge Village, Massachusetts *40*
On Visiting Wordsworth 41
Pondering a Duck, Ueno Gardens, Tokyo 42
    A duck and turtle squabble, Ueno Gardens, Tokyo *43*
A Three Kingdoms Story 44
Jungle Book 45
    I. The Road 45
    II. The Village 46
    III. The Streambed 47
    IV. Tiger-Shape 48
    V. The Water Beside the River 49
    VI. The Forest 50

VII. The Underground...51
    Praying mantis, Rancho Bernardo, California *52*
From Kabul to Kandahar...53
Valley in Ancash..54
    I. 54
    II. 55
    III. 56
    IV. 57
Modus ponens...58
Apples 59
Driveways..60
Peace 61
London Squall..62
    Feather fallen in King's Square, London *62*
Afternoon Joggers 63
Watching a Play 64
Life Before Light 65
    Power lines, Jacksonville, Florida *65*
Eves..66
48..67
Circadian 68
The Clock Before Falling Asleep..69
Herbie Hancock on a Headache 70
Departures 71
    The Miraflores Lighthouse, Lima, Peru *71*
Lullabye: Waking Dream 72
Working Late 73
Earthquakes and Oceans..74
Anywhere 75
Life and Love 76
Caledonian Creation Myth...77
I Saw and Heard..78
    Seagull, Santa Monica Pier *79*
Logomachia..80
[citation needed] 81
The State of Poetry..82
Spiderwebs in Dew...83
Diminuendo...84

Guitar headstock *85*
24 Views of Mt. Fuji 86
Nude Descending a Staircase 88
Guernica 90
Paradise Shark 91
Since the Zombies Came 92
Soul Food 93
Out of Water 94
Swans in Lake Zurich, Switzerland *95*
The Dragons and Me 96
Goety 97
The Pangrammatic Fox 98
Flicker 99
The Age of the Computer Poem 100
Network Optimization 101
Ode to Code: A Geek Poem 102
The BASICs of life 104
Puzzle Poetry 105
When is a Rhyme a Rhyme? 106
If you… 107
For Every Fiddle Found 108

Notes 110
Balloon over Rancho Santa Fe, California *110*
About the Author 127

Foreword

For many years, I posted a poem on my blog on Sundays.

Back when I was in graduate school earnestly studying to be a better poet, my advisor told me that my poetry was hermetic, self-referential, and never likely to be the sort of poetry that reaches many people. I wanted to write poems that connected with everyone—populist poems, not just poems for myself.

As these Sunday Poems were written and posted on my blog, I found myself writing to and for that blog audience: largely folks who came there for discussion of games and the game industry, who had little or no interest in poetry.

Some of the poems I posted were older poems; most of them were newly written that day. Many of them were responses to whatever I had read or experienced that week. Often, poems were prompted by the reader's comments or challenges.

Some of them were read by a few thousand people, then forgotten. Some very few clicked with their tiny audience, and went mildly viral (for a poem) on the Internet.

Here they are now, gathered up. I was never able to submit them to magazines, because by posting them on the Internet, I had irretrievably damaged their already non-existent commercial viability or academic creditability.

⌘

Many of these poems originally had hyperlinks throughout them. I have provided endnotes instead. These are largely drawn from the blog posts that tended to accompany each poem. I apologize if they simply go on to explain what I was thinking and rob the poem of whatever mystique it might have possessed. I indicate whether a given poem has an endnote using this symbol by the poem's title: ✤

Originally, several of these poems came accompanied by photographs. In place of that, there are pen and ink drawings. The illustrations were mostly done digitally, based on photographs I have taken on my travels.

I will likely post more at some point. You never know. You can visit http://www.raphkoster.com to check and see.

✤

What follows is my original post, written in October 2005, launching the series on my blog.

The Sunday Poem (original introduction)

In another life, I was a poet. If it's possible to stop being a poet. Or if one's life has intermediate lives. Or something. Quite likely, the most useless piece of paper I own is the one that actually *certifies* me as a poet. A truly ludicrous idea. Of course, this particular certificate, which comes in the form of a diploma giving me an MFA in creative writing, is nonetheless carefully kept in a leather binder at the bottom of a closet, because to do otherwise would be to admit something unpleasant about how I spent multiple years of my life.

Most poems sit in drawers never to be read, and that is a good fate for most poems, really, because most poems aren't really written for others to read. I think the certificate means that the poems I wrote are supposed to actually get read. But currently they do not get read; they instead sit in a virtual drawer on my hard drive.

I have an audience these days; depending on where I write, it can be quite a large audience. On the blog, not so much, but heck, if I post on certain game websites, I get audiences in the tens of thousands. At times, within certain games, I have had audiences in the hundreds of thousands. Most poets have audiences that are rather small.

Odds are you could care less about poetry. I once cared passionately about it, but as with many past passions, it is difficult to remember the *why* of it. It's a fact that is there, but that is difficult to understand anymore, like a lapsed religion or a forgotten mania for collecting something.

But since you are my small audience, and these poems will never be sent to the *New Yorker* because I no longer have the passion, and because I suspect that there are more people willing to read poems on the Internet than there are total people reading the *New Yorker*, I am going to post the poems I was once passionate about here on this website. One every Sunday, and they shall be called "The Sunday Poem." They will have their own category, and people who are interested in poetry can click on just that category and read them, and people who could not care less can skip them.

What's more, they will have comments open, and I will actually answer questions and comments. You never got to do that with Emily Dickinson or Poe or Milton, so you can look upon this as your chance for revenge if you dislike poetry.

Many of these poems have stories behind them. I may post those too.

I rarely write new poems these days. But I have many many older ones.

If I miss a Sunday, be sure to beat me up.

✤ Why It Is Hard

We always write our verses on the green.
Extolling nature, one dull paean, then
Another, the savannah evo psych
So loves a bellwether to our brains.

We hammer home our thoughts of death, with odes
And eulogies, our writing full of black,
Of wistfulness, of melancholy. Sad,
As if mere "sad" was "deep" and "deep" was "good."

We speak of love, the thrust, surrender, catch
Of breath, exchange of fluids, the coy glance
And longing. Each of us forgets that all
Of us know all of this. Forever. Now.

So much of writing tells us what we know.
So much of culture trades old comforts, myths
We tell ourselves to keep the strange away.
Just three great subjects, and our story's done.

This makes it hard to write each Sunday poem.

✤ Pistachio

Pistachio piled high, a green the shade of leaves in shade;
Scintilla sparkles, specular sliding off the cone.

A spritz of soda, carbon captured, bubbles bursting;
Antiseptic odor effervescing from the glass.

Water stains on spoons, overlapping nebulae. Straws. Scoops.
Color buckets, congealed craters, rough gorges. Crème.

Here there is no death except in melting. There is no love,
But for the sharing of banana splits, there is no nature

Save for green the shade of leaves in shade, the nuts,
The flavor on the tongue, purchased by my grandpa.

We chrome, we swirl, we pile double-high, we watch
As scoops sizzle on the hot cement, fallen from their perch.

Candy

A single stagnant drop of sugar, caught and coalesced and cooked to crystal
    shine.
It's fricative and fresh, this lump or lolly, taffy, toffee, gumdrop, goo or fairy
    dust.
It conjures summers, jujubes and dimes. A stick of pixie, lips of wax, and time
To race about, the dog at heel, the swarm of kids, the tinkling ice cream
    truck, the sweat.

The sweet is sharp; your tongue gets bumps. A crack can catch your gums, cut
    you, leave wounds as small
As any cut inside your mouth: enormous, one more thing to suck on,
    strawberry.
We face the same choice of every day: to crunch would be to hurry it along.
It's sweeter far to savor sweets and time before the time and sweets are soft,
    then gone.

Suomi

Finnish girls flying flagpole tall,
Scarves bannering their backs.
Overalls, engineers, bottles and booze,
Everyone sporting white tasseled caps.
Balloon constellations float children to sea,
Ice cream left melting by frozen degrees,
Puffiny birds held back by the wind and
Licorice pipes and smoke from elk grilled.
A moment of city before scattering to cabins
To hide among birches and in kitchen gatherings.
Gather they must to celebrate May
Even if May is not quite awake.
Winter must end, Suomi insists, for winter
Is nothing when summer's at stake.

Geese seen from Kaivopuisto, Helsinki

After Serious Sunburn

Stippled red striated speckles buttered deep
In cocoa, aloe; the slide of cloth on skin
Searing scars of sun and sand.

Skin in sheets, shed sly like sidewinds
Scrubbing rocks, sloughing like cicadas,
Scattered food for mites.

So starts the metamorphose, stretching
To a higher self, a sentience sophisticated
Now for SPFs of sixty-plus.

❧ The Road to Whimsy

We're half the way to Whimsy. Our feet are getting sore.
Half the way to Whimsy, where we plan to open doors.

Butterflies the size of bats hover 'round our heads
And bicycles on bouncy roads have sparkles on their treads.

Half the way to Whimsy is only partly droll
But at least we're finding it a pleasant little stroll.

Ahead a man is hawking; his bird gives us a glare.
When walking down to Whimsy it doesn't do to stare.

And at the gates of Whimsy we stop and take a gander.
The gates are icon-clad and people crowd the landing.

Inside the gates of Whimsy you're not allowed to eat.
If you spill the beans, you see, they may not let you leave.

And photographs? Heavens forfend! That isn't why you came!
The denizens are not the sort to fit inside a frame.

If I described—the robots, lights, the watercolored gears,
The shelves of books, daguerreotypes, boxes full of tears,

The flock of sparrows, spider's web, the flavor of ice cream—
Oh, never mind. Just pretend you're visiting a dream.

And when you're leaving Whimsy, remember: no one stays.
Most folks visit briefly, and rarely in their days.

Pack a wistful smile for lunch, and wear your smallest clothes.
You can ride the cat bus home, to rest your tired toes.

Slide

There's
A pile of sand
Backyard, all covered in snow;
We perch on the very top and slide to collide into
A panting heap of children, red noses and colds.

Science Homework

Cabbage juice and acid a pinkish fluid make.
Cabbage juice staying blue means you found a base.
Cabbage juice with bleach, though, is turning green;
Heavens! A chemical reaction unforeseen.

Glasses strewn on kitchen table, tablespoons of love,
Careful mixing of antacids and the smelly stuff;
We tolerate the messes and hope nothing explodes
For sake of experiments further down the road.

Avogadro's number has nothing much to tell us
Here on a Sunday while younger brother's jealous.
"I want to blow stuff up!" he says; someday his chance will come.
Meanwhile, I ladle cabbage juice into a poem.

If only we each got six glasses for our mixtures.
But all our lives are made of tests that became our fixtures.
Hypothesize, trial run, measure and record;
You take the acid, form your base, and keep on moving forward.

✤ Sometimes a Duck is Just a Duck
(A Semi-Sonnet On Whether Strategy Guides Are Cheating)

Suppose you had a duck to deconstruct.
It sits atop a log, it quacks at things,
It flaps its wings all frantic, daring, dumb.
What parts of duck are really duck, you think?

Take feet. They're webbed, for sure, and orange-black.
But geese and other cousins have them too.
That is not duckness, any more than spoon-
Billed beakness is a sign this duck is true.

It might reside in quacking; ducks take pride
In never shutting up. Perhaps parades
Of ducklings crossing streets like in old books?
A duck of culture, a consensus made,

Composites made of pieces sharp and blunt.
I must conclude that ducks are… elephants.

❖ The Piano Teacher's House

The tops of ornamented lintels, carved
With bevels, claw-feet foyer tables caught
In dust: a prelude silk and parquet smooth
Where children march to pianistic doom.

Cliché: the piano almost seems alive,
An ungainly odd-bellied creature, lip
Drawn tight to hide teeth ebony and white.
Lace doilies seem like distraught hair a-flop.

Above, the upper hallway boasts a boa,
A feather flutter nailed to a frame,
A Decca seven eight, velvet ribbons,
The sound of Scaramouche and Lindy Hop.

Pinned to the broken mirror, an autograph
Now faded: Mario Lanza. Perky hats
To wear on bobbed short flapper hair.
A photo torn in half.

With faces veiled, the spare room mannequins
Who turn translucent eyes to see, discuss
The latest news from Paris, the day they earn
Their legs, and when the music sets them free.

⚜ Davey Flower Becomes a Pterodactyl

"Raaaaak! Awrrrk! Kraaa! Urrgg!" I heard from down the hall,
A piercing, plaintive, prehistoric sort of call.

"What's going on?" I called out, and soon my wife replied.
"Your son's become a pterodactyl. Seriously. No lie."

It's true indeed—our little boy, our blue-eyed Davey Flower
Had become an awkward, flapping, pointy dinosaur.

His sister promptly cheered and laughed, the bratty little wench.
"Yay, my baby brother's gone!" then whined about the stench.

And as he tried to flap his wings, she quickly wondered too,
"Maybe could he do tricks like the parrot at the zoo?"

His mother started out concerned, but quickly justified it
As punishment for messy rooms and making her so tired.

What do you feed a pterodactyl? He's got goldfish from the tank!
No, don't eat the hamster too! And put down baby Frank!

Chicken fingers, popcorn, fries. Figures, some things never change,
That's all he'd eat before too! Even then we thought it strange.

Davey gained more energy at whatever rate we lost it.
It wore off around midnight, when we were just exhausted.

By then he'd mastered flapping, and hovering in place,
And started eyeing windows, contemplating outer space.

Now he's grown, and when I ask if he recalls those days,
He says, while diapering his kid, "It was just a phase."

But I wonder if he dreams at night and maybe sort of cries.
I still do when I recall my blue-eyed son once knew the way to fly.

Sierras From Above

From heights we learn that nothing's very high.
These seams on earth, as raised as stitching, are
The tyranny of gravity made wry.

The mountains: hands, folded and folded, turf
Brown hand upon hand upon hand twined overlapping,
Quiescent, senescent under blanket earth.

Softback, spineback, brokeback, extruded round;
All life, from here, is mold discoloring
Rock, a growth that could be wiped away.

There is a loneliness where aquifers
Reach spindled fingers in the lightning of
Erosion, and do not touch.

✤ Clouds from Above

Honoring all the clichés,
Evanescing like cottony candy,
Like cotton itself, soft twists torqued,
Tangled, aloft with imagined
Wild dragons—their qualia lie:

Our visions, our worships,
Are tepid, not rapid, have ice
In their bellies, not fire.

As we claw our way,
Damp and surrounded, through
Serpentine guts, grim gray tangles
Of mist, I see Tintagel's battle
Is fought yet again:

We are lords of the sky;
We have burst from our stone;
This is dynasty.

✤ Descending to the Airport at Night

Marine layer fog a glacier over cities:
For once the sea is higher than the land.
This is the deepest darkest ocean trench,
our plain, our towns, drowned in atmosphere.

We move insensible upon this sea bed
as fluorescent, incandescent fish.
Scattered jewels, sodden treasure jostled
by unknown eddies, unscoped physics,

the science of the currents, systems of
the waves, the sins of sociology,
the breathless and the brave reduced to just
a coral-tracing spattering. A crust.

Salmon coursing off to breed,
a billion gaping mouths to feed,
territories mostly small,
traces barely there at all
once abrading water has its way
and softens all our brights to gray.

From this all life was born.
The sum. The sea. The salt.
We gasp, we dart. We flow.
Exalt.

Under microscope, from a beachhead far away
We are each as special as a grain of sand.

We are each as special as a grain of sand
Under microscope.

SUNDAY POEMS

San Diego from Presidio Park

❖ If Trees Did Not Stop Growing

The trees are dense with cellulose,
are grasses overgrown. They fork
the sky, they prize the stratosphere

And if they got there, what?

Leaves freeze & cause a late-fall snow
The jet stream buffets branches, snap!
Planes would dodge and fearful birds would fly
their nests grown far too high

Beyond, the stars, the dark, the places
no trees know, the airless empty, bright
the beeping satellites, the sight of meteorites
that risk their crowns afire

Upper reaches made of silver
Treehouses of gold
Brittle twigs and filigree
swaying in the cold

The green forgot
the sun a harsh unending glare
One beauty traded to another
buds that cannot bear

From the moon, the Earth a feathered ball
a-bristle with the tall, the trees that reached
and sought, the trees that got beyond

Where Mother Nature never got

❖ Driving to Tainan

I came all this way to visit New Jersey:
Blank concrete barriers under smog,
Highways robed in rice paddies.
Granaries coated in rust rust
Idly. Trade rice for more
American grains, and this drive
Is one more trip through waste, waste
Of nature, of wild.

The city Tainan is strokes
And motorcycles, a rush to buy
And sell. Here, there, everywhere
Adolescents gather, girls to giggle,
Guys to pretend.

Down an alley we find a square,
An empty lot loomed by cosmetics ads.
Plastic sheeting circles plastic tables,
A sizzle of shells, sashimi and squid.
The fish eyes are everywhere, and
Taiwan beer tastes very familiar:
Perhaps there is only one beer, and many bottles.

A man at the next table is,
For a moment, my friend Will, the artist,
In every detail but eyes,
Hair, beard, chin, cheeks.
The recognition of his laugh makes me
Laugh, so I inhale differences
To exhale similarities.

So, then: there is no where, there.
There is only who, and when,
And why, and the answer
Is always.

✤ Lions in Vegas

There are lions in the middle of Vegas.
They sleep on plastic floors, and hunt nothing
To the chimes of endless treasure.

They prowl fifty acres of air, they take us
By surprise, but work six hour shifts,
These lions in the middle of Vegas.

A grand bubble in the middle of a bubble
At the edge of a bubble in the middle of a desert,
Ostentatious signs of endless treasure.

Outside, the predators chase fickleness,
Count odds and error. Everyone is watched
Watching the lions in the middle of Vegas.

When you reach the river, the lions lurk
Waiting on the other side, hungry,
Jealous guardians of their shiny treasure.

Whose entertainment is whose?
Which bubble is likely to break us?
We play lions in the middle of Vegas
But are prey to dreams of chiming treasure.

❖ A Cherufe Tale

Ay, Pedro de Valdivia, of Extremadura,
Do you miss your granite home?
The Bío Bío shores are flat and muddy waters
And Mapuches lurk in bushes and in loam.

Last night the cry of the Chonchón, *tué tué tué,*
Called out bad luck for you and Spain.
Do you fear for your fresh-made town of Concepción?
It will survive, as you survived the Atacama plain.

Tomorrow you will drink your gold, molten hot,
And writhe your guts out on a stake.
Your foster son Lautaro is now the native general
And you will die, hidalgo, one betrayed.

The Pillan spirits of this land have anointed you,
Pedro de Valdivia, rude conquistador.
Your small town will one day speak the word
"Independence" in the Plaza Mayor.

You were the last of knights, you loved the last of queens.
Your European tale is Spanish no more.
It matters not if once you were of Extremadura,
Cherufe sacrifice; you die a myth Chilean born.

Boston Photographs

There is a street in Boston where the gas lamps have been burning
For a hundred forty years; where lamplighters no longer walk
The cycle of the twenty four, since globule mantles left to glow
Were cheaper than the labor spent in dimming gas in rain and snow.

The gravestones at the Granary are sunk in mud, or shattered sheets.
The midnight ride of Paul Revere is heaps of rocks, is piles
Of pennies, and a rain soaked flag or two. The Burying Ground
Is older still, and the thousands share five hundred weathered stones.

A Custom House is a hotel. A macaroni bursts in yellow sculpture
Beside a Market square. A Brutalist town hall juts jaws beside
Stark glass memorials and Boston's oldest pub. They said, "You can't
Hear city sounds from inside Boston Common!" but they lied.

Look!—homes upon a fisher wharf, held up by mussels and stout wood,
The Charles for a cellar door and a neighbor in a sloop.
With California earthquake eyes, the pilings underneath the wharf
That hold the condominiums high are trembling on the edge of hope.

We watch the tide; the rise, the fall, the six foot gap from tall to small.
The fixity of history, the folly of infinity, the way the town believes itself
The sailing ship, the catamaran, the hackneys and velocipedes,
The ferry, horses, cabs and cars, the moving van, and the rumbling T,

Four hundred years all held as close as simultaneity.
Mistaken hills hold monuments to battles fought elsewhere,
And staid New England poets paint their copperplated iambs
In pixels on a screen, declaiming beats from Faneuil Hall.

I cast these Boston photographs to what they once called ether,
Where they may last as long as tiny mantles glow.
They are the fixity of touristry, the river banks we made by hand,
Are monuments as long as networks grow, as long as human power flows;
Are structures standing strong upon the sand.

❖ All Stories Are Like This

Pliny tells a story of a ghost who wished his bones dug up;
He came at night, a haunt and clanking spirit, chained,
To scare the renters out of his apartment in the night.

But a philosopher, he took the spot, since it was cheap,
And worked till late at night. Clanking was obnoxious,
So when the ghost appeared, he made it wait.

Finally, his letters done, he rose and marked the spot
Where the skeleton arose bechained from garden plot.
The next day, of course, a putrid corpse was found.

Pliny himself, much less said philosoph, are much alike;
Both beyond their moldering days, living only in the write.
And yet, who reads Pliny? None. Athenodorus? Who?

Somewhere there's a garden plot where ancient Romans rise,
And clank their way to knock on busy students' doors.
Each serves as Pliny to his ghost, mostly for a grade.

And here I serve as Pliny too, retelling ancient renters' tales
Because my fancy caught upon the grave; if Pliny can't,
Then must I create small verse to be a ghost for you.

❧ Building the Globe

We heft the oak beams, one two three, each count
A sturdy truss; smooth hewn and splintered, blunt
And heavy, painted gaily marbled, dun

And costumeless. By numbers shall we know
Their place, when Southwark greets our lumber load;
The Theatre is no more, and soon we'll have a Globe.

In Shoreditch now there stands a hole, on lease-
Land Burbage didn't own. And past the trees,
By open fields, his Men will have a Streete-

Built O, wherein proud Oberon will prance
And Lear cry out his woe; where faery dance
For groundlings' sake, and Puck plays out his pranks.

We'll sift the straw and lay it straight on top,
And paint anew the spangled sky aloft
Above proscenium's boards. We'll stop

The crowd with good stout rails, so high-pitch boys
Can stain their lips and flounce their tails, and raise
A ruckus to the skies, the center of our noise.

But first, we must dismantle, first we take
Apart. If all the world's a stage and planks
Are how it's made, then for our Good Lord's sake

I hope he spent his seven days as well,
Assembling worlds in beams of thirty ells,
A Shakespere for his script, Queen Bess, and all
A-toiling midst the sound of London's bells.

⚜ Dead Media

The past is always umbers and ochres, faded colors, pastels and creams.
Statues gone bone white as pigments all flake and leave behind blank marbled
    dreams.
It's black and white movies with scratches, Polaroid snaps yellowed and bare,
Unsmiling faces with minute exposures and cave daubings now barely there.

Today seems like it's all vivid colors. Today, we assume thirty two bits.
The shadings of grayscale are stylistic choices; the resolution, as high as will fit.
Our dots per inch are far more fragile than carnelian, purple and woad:
When erasure comes, as it always does, we'll have nothing magnetic to show.

And then will our children look back in wonder? Amazed at the lack of it all?
Not just color, but shape, form and measure, evanescent bitrotted walls.
They'll build abstruse theories of absent aesthetics, or tell funny tales of fools
Who thought lightning and sand a stable canvas and pixels permanent tools.

Candy II

Imagine

If we preserved our memories in candies... each one, each flavor,
Releasing a specific other time back into our minds.
Bags of winter nights all minty fresh, first kisses, that time you skinned your
    knee.
The painful days would slice your tongue that candy way.
The days we don't recall would be the ones we ate unconscious,
Half a bagful disappeared without our noticing.
Rich chocolate of love, the peppermint of anger,
The anise rum of jealous rage, the coconut of sorrow.
We'd grow bloated on the past.

Some memories, like any other memory, would surface
From the cushions of a couch, sticky, pasted over
Dust and hair and scraps of paper wrapping, and we'd hold them
Pondering whether they are sweet, or just the flavor of regret.

✤ The Spencer Wheelhouse

Enough's been written now about old 97,
The way she rushed downhill to reach the Spencer Yards,
How she ran the rails ragged off the Stillhouse Trestle
And died a steamer's death, splinters all afire.

But not enough is said about the men of Spencer town,
Where the broken locomotive came to be repaired;
The wheelhouse 'round the turntable held her shattered heart
And men of Rowan County stood around her and prepared.

Listen for the hissing of the water at 180,
Scalding hot and stinking of the grease, the lye, the soap.
Watch the molten metal be pounded back to 4-6-0,
The heaving of the cranes, the burning of the ropes.

Three shifts of hours eight, five and three sixty days a year,
Three quarters of the town held the Spencer jobs down tight
And sent their children to the Shops, to work the Southern line,
To keep the romance of the rail running steaming hot and right.

And Spencer's families stood proud, invested in their rails.
Then diesel came. The town, it died. The years of boom are gone.
The locomotive 97, she was melted down for scrap
And Spencer's work was lost, whatever you might hear in songs.

Today just a museum stands, the boxcars lanky orange rust
And empty echo wheelhouse halls full of dining cars and dust.
That is how the steamers died: not boom, but economic bust;
As Spencer's men learned that rails, and steam, and all the dreams entailed
Are things that you can love, but cannot really trust.

✤ Change of Dreams

We have no more Sargasso Sea:
We've lost the tales from *Argosy,*
Of giant jewfish swallowing divers
And ghost ship press gangs snaring live ones.

No more stalks the sleuth in alleys,
Nor with Sumatran rats he dallies.
Murders ceased to be genteel,
And duels settle sans cold steel.

So rarely see we Poe-like horrors;
Our monsters are our mundane neighbors.
We do not live in R'lyeh's streets
But kids must stay within ten feet,

While half the way to Paradise
The trash collects, a plastic isle.
A new Atlantis or Hy Breasil,
A continent recycled and eternal.

❖ Maid Marian

Oh Marian maid, queen of May, born a shepherd girl!
What have they done? Your flock is gone,
Your ballad's of a different world.
Once you stood alone, you know—you were not just a foil,
But instead you played the central maid
As Yorkshire festivals you toiled.

And then dependency came in, for propriety's sake,
For maids alone cannot be shown
Lest women proper place mistake.
French, then Saxon, poor and back to Norman blood,
You stood apart and pined your heart
For loves you never needed much.

Your love, your shepherd boy, now lord made rough outlaw.
Your good French name Leaford became,
And you an archery prize for all?
From play to film and back again, your shape a-shift and formless raw,
And now you're dead as roles are shed
And actors move through dialogue.

Do you wander alleys now, and shop at big box stores?
Do you worry mortgages, or giving to the poor?
Your ballad flows and we all know that stories grow and change and more;
You may have spent some time with bad boy Robin Hood
But given time the shepherdess will be back home in her own wood.
Marian is always there in thought, be she queen of May or not.

✤ Amelia on Nikumaroro

"This is Amelia Earhart. Ship is on a reef south of the equator."—heard by Dana Randolph of Rock Springs, Wyoming, via shortwave radio

Itasca, Itasca, why won't you come in?
Two days, Noonan sick, and now the plane's a-tilt,
The engine dipping wet to the lagoon.
Soon the salty sea will get in, and then
The radio charge will sink, disconnecting, and silt
Will swallow this Electra, our signal's tomb.

When I was little Meeley, the girl in brown,
I read my books and walked alone, and swore
To be myself, not just a skirt and pretty eyes.
But I still doled out medicines to men struck down
Before the Armistice, in Toronto during the War.
And now I tend the ill again, in paradise.

It's hard to escape. A life spent moving now at rest
On the 157/337 line, adrift
A thousand miles from my own place and time.
A chance to be myself, for some years at least.
To camp, crack clams, light fires, desperately sift
Through sandy logbooks for hints of where I went awry.

I can't help but think my lovely red Vega
Would have held me up, buffeted by wind and sun,
Wings cupped like hands, beseeching.
Instead, I had to reach for a new plane, the way
I always have since I asked Anita Snook in '21
"I want to fly. Will you teach me?"

If you can hear me, this is A.E. on a reef,
South of the equator. Noonan's fading, I am forsook,
With no place to dig a grave. I stand on coral,
A yards-wide strand planes buzz but do not see.
I have lived my life reaching for the history books.
I will not stand my life to have a death with no moral.

Itasca, why won't you come in?
Was my final flight into the sun?

Why Wulfric Lived to 90

"The third guy from the left, along the trestle board,
Who drank a bit more mead than strictly needed… *Him,*
The one with orange hair and braids all down to here.

Yeah, that's the guy. He slept through the whole thing, the jerk.
When Grendel came and ripped our arms and popped our skulls,
He slid, plain drunk, right under the roast pig, and snored.

I want his saga privileges revoked. I won't
Put up with crap like this. Last time we slew a drake,
He *tripped.* What sort of hero trips on dragon tails?

He makes us all look bad. So yank him from the books.
Declare him warg, or extirpate him from the band.
We've got our quest to finish; he just holds us back."

Poor Wulfric, all Valhalla will not sing his name.

But grandkids might.

Reactions to the Awful News

I. The Preacher

Poor Jenny Blade she spent her days
Whistling with her teakettles,
Humming tunes in bare wood rooms
And watching crop dust settle.
The sun fell hot on what was not
Quite a shabby little farm
And Jenny Blade sweated and stayed
And did no one no harm.
But in the dark, her country heart
Pounding fast and narrow,
Jenny rubbed and drew her blood
And lit up bone and marrow.
A true believer, in her fever,
In God and all the devils,
She was sure she was not pure
And was destined down to Hell.
And when she dozed with windows closed
And shades all drawn up tight,
She swore the air was filled with fair
And frightful demons of the night.
So poor Jenny Blade died today—
The funeral is tomorrow.
I feel no loss but I'll raise a cross
And pretend to feel some sorrow;
While she haunts the steam, all gaunt,
Shifting, serrated, whistling, brave,
An edgy film of smoke and will,
That sinning ghost of Jenny Blade!

II. Mother Martin

So my spinster sister swept her soul
And fell into a grave?
I told Jonas weeks ago
She was looking peaked. God save
Her weary bones! Lord knows
She slaved enough, she worked hard
To keep herself alive! When the land won't grow
And people treat you hardly
Decent, you get to thinking,
What if I moved
Away from this damn town? It's sinking
Into prejudice, anyhow. When it can't be proved
Nohow that a husband's needed
To grow the corn or cook the meal,
Then Lord knows she was a saint, and no bleedin'
Parson or reactionary snot kid'll
Tell me otherwise! No, they can't,
Not me, a widow since they was babes piddlin'
In their pants.

III. The Shopkeeper

She paid her bills on time,
Always to the cent. Each week
She bought some milk, some salt,
Sugar for her candies,
Meal for all the ducks.
Her credit was good, and I
'Spect whoever gets her farm
Will have good credit too.

A farm in snow, Jefferson, Maryland

IV. The Teacher

A bad example to the kids and that,
But good Lord what a mind!
She thought as fast as rattlers
Strike, for all she was half blind.
She'd seen a lot in this here town
In her half century and some.
When she was younger she came around
Whenever the kids were going home.
She'd watch them walk along and after
Be able to tell me which had failed
The quiz that day, which had laughter
Like bells on dancing shoes, which trailed
The class in spelling "February" and which
Was beaten by his folks. I swear,
If I wasn't educated I'd say she was a witch.
But that's not here nor there, I daresay.

V. The Boy

I found her, sirs, I did, I did,
Rocking, talking in her rocking chair,
Talking well after she was dead!
The chair it moved and grooves were worn
In floor flat by her feet, and her tongue
Ran along like it never did
Before she was deceased. The stink
Was something fearful, thinking back,
And back inside the house the
Smell was stronger than manure.
Her eyes were shut but the eyes they bulged
And her feet were bare and blue
And red—and I ran yelling out
"Watch out! Watch out! She's still talking,
But old Jenny Blade is dead!"

VI. Mrs. Shay

I had no truck with the likes of her.
I've got nothing to say.
My husband thought her horse was nice,
But she wouldn't sell for what he'd pay.

VII. Old Crow

When she wore a gown it soared
And swung like feathers on a bird.
When she danced she twirled her feet
And tapped out rhythms no one heard.
When she was young Miss Jennifer
She cooked a meal or two for me,
We chatted all the night. Dower
Be damned! said I, but Father
Said money really mattered.
So she went unwed and I went on
And married Ellen, whose ashes now are scattered.
Now Jenny's gone and soon so will I
And the old ones will have vanished,
Ah Ellen! Even you have vanished,
Even you have vanished…

VIII. The Fellow with the Suit

Who the hell was Jenny Blade?
And why the devil care?
She's laid to rest, it's for the best—
She hadn't flesh to spare.
I'm just passing through, you know,
I never knew the gal.
But if you'd like me to show
A token sorrow, then hell!
I'm sorry—now, can we talk
About the loan and contract
And why Jasper balks
At giving me my money back?

IX. Jenny

Whistling, mumbling, rocking in my chair,
I talked with ghosts and people not quite there
And now that I have passed away, my cot
Lies empty bare, and the sun is not as hot
On my thin neck, I feel alive again, ready
To take on worlds again, even dead,
To twirl and dance again, to be what I
Had never been, to laugh and hate and cry
Again, to get past the shallow shade
That I'd become, a person entirely made
Of other's opinions of who was Jenny Blade.

Opinions and lives always fade.

X.

Goodbye, Miss Jennifer, take your bows
And hope they shut the door when you leave,
Turn out the light,
Close the gate,
And someone remembers to feed the cows.

Storeroom barrels, Old Sturbridge Village, Massachusetts

✢ On Visiting Wordsworth

In a half-constructed sheepfold above old Green-head Ghyll
There lies a skeleton, with 'Michael' written on its stone.
The grass has fed upon his flesh and the dew has drunk its fill
But people stay away, afraid of thinking that the shepherd died alone.

Oh, Michael, roll up this land and put it in your pocket,
Then walk away from Green-head Ghyll and give it to your son.
Then the sun will miss the grazing grass and fall on barren rock
And I will walk along the hills without regret for what has gone.

Pondering a Duck, Ueno Gardens, Tokyo

Say you have a duck, and the duck is daring,
A frantic quacking fowl that disturbs the water's peace.
Would it pick a quarrel with placid turtles drowsing?
Would it raise a ruckus and disturb the carp asleep?

Of course it would. Some critters quack whole days away,
Heedless of the peace a summer garden brings.
They cannot help but lack the sense to meditate,
Their temper dragging them from windy cry to whim.

Compare, contrast, the carp beneath,
Always moving, never loud.
They gape their mouths to beg for food,
But do not bellow when they crowd.

Above them sit the lily pads, the waterstriding bugs,
The people at their temples, the tourists on their days.
The lake itself enduring, patient, with towers 'round it rung.
The duck you see, just visits. The turtle comes to pray.

A duck and turtle squabble, Ueno Gardens, Tokyo

✤ A Three Kingdoms Story

The wise man sits in the Three Kingdoms story
Playing music on his lap harp.
The wise man sits in the Three Kingdoms story
On castle walls, to make the siege
That rages shorter, casual
Though all is discontent.
The wise man sits in the Three Kingdoms story
And I am sitting on a park bench
By his park-bound monument.
Around me past the stone park fence
Taipei grumbles, heaves, and shakes, but
The wise man sits in the Three Kingdoms story
Playing music on his lap harp
And I am listening

✤ Jungle Book

I. The Road

The jungle breathes
with its own rhythms
for its own reasons.

The road is a knife cut
parting the jungle
and no use can claim it
from its source.

Ghosts jabber among the thick-veined leaves
Panthers dream of standing over campfires
Jowls sag over flames and sparks

This road is a gullet
into some animal too vast
to comprehend.

II. The Village

A small village sits like a patch of sanity
In the center of a wilderness fenced out
But it dreams of singeing the tiger's whiskers

The thick jungle sweeps to the grazing-grounds
And stops there cut off by a hoe
Kept from the little gullies and scrabbly grass

Herds disappear into the wrinkled ravines
To wallow in mud pools in the scrub
Where they can dip their mighty heads into the mud

Eyes begin to close as the sun beats India
And the only sounds are the cries of the kites
And the constant *zuuummm* of the flies

The big blue buffalo spray mud and water
Gazing around with heavy brown eyes
As it drips down cavernous nostrils

Mud cakes on the nilghai and cracks
Into river deltas on their backs
They dream of singeing the tiger's whiskers

The land is a blanket of rocky ground cover
Draped on boulders bumpy and misshapen
The soil has melted onto the bones of the earth

The cows and you yourself walk on it like flies
No tail comes from heaven to swat you
And as the buffalo break free of mud the crack!

It must be like gunshots on a gray evening
Red-gold flowers bursting from every branch
Tonight the souls of tigers are dead
And the whiskers are ashes kept in lacquered boxes.

III. The Streambed

Moss on all sides
   Rock iridescent green
 Dark rusty brown
   Water drips with a tap
     Tap tap tap
    The stream is dry
   But water flows across leaves
     Dew trails trail
   Streambed lined with rocks
      Head sized round rocks
    Held in place with plants
     Like green sprays
       Water crashing against
    A coast a cliff a cranny
   Walking on the skulled
    Rocks the ant path
  Trickles the trail
   Fuzz on plant stalks
     Shifts lights and shadow
   And foliage whispers
  The green takes over
  The world and everything
 Is shaped like leaves
  Like stalks like roots
  Like the spaces
   Between plants
 A wreck of rock tumbled
Like a heap of pebbles
  Pried greenfingers
 Leave mortar pulled
  From rock and rock
Nothing is left here
  But the Poison
 People
a whirl
wind
 of
thorns

IV. Tiger-Shape

I hear the ancient creaking of trees too mighty
to support themselves tonight, the tired cackling
of monkeys, like men grown too old to understand
the world, or to stop pretending that they had, once.

There is whispering of water dripping from cupped leaves
far in the canopy, as it passes from bough to bark
in a procession of hands that do not touch, streaking
stripes of silver through the air as it shines and beads.

Creepers dangle pliant and slender, lianas that brush
my shoulders when I struggle through them, breaking
the vines and painting myself with yellow sap,
sticky and oozing down my forehead, marking me.

The tiger's stripes were painted thus, when he
ran through the creepers one night, panicking
and stretching his sore muscles as far as they could
go, the night without a moon that he killed Man.

And now springy grass cushions my feet, ribbed
woody stalks of bamboo reach to catch the birds,
and a web of plants holds the whole thing together,
binding me in my yellow stripes, a shadow and a shape.

Knoll to log to stone, small hollows hide the chiya fox,
sly and hooded cobras, the cowering Indian sambhur,
and though this fallen log is a banquet for the insects
tonight the moon is a hole, and I must go hunting.

V. The Water Beside the River

The sun makes its green-filtered way down past leaves.
Clouds scud when the Waingunga is not high enough.

Rocks grind and grumble current in the depths.
The breeze hackles necks and scatters mosquitoes.

The water at the edges is hidden by lily pads and leaves.
Some are dark brown and others a sickly vibrant green.

Insects skate across the water as if it were glass.
Sketchy ripples slide away from their pockmark feet.

Damp velvet water slides cold and oily against skin.
Feet feel the whispery touches of waterlily roots.

A wild plantain stretches out its sharp triangular leaf.
Where it touches the water it sends out ripples like explorers.

VI. The Forest

The trees stand apart from each other,
afraid to come too close,
trunks worn smooth by the streams of wolves coursing past them
and the scratching deer.

Smooth columns: this is a cathedral of trees,
a place of arches and infinite doorways
formed by branches curving silently into the air.

Stained stars hang from the vaulted boughs:
flowers of wax,
candles burning with inner light,
exuding scents and marble incense.

A place of worship where hapless trees are choked
with glacial trailing patience
until the massed weight of coils makes arches creak
in the spring rains, when elephants bellow.

Then the bough breaks
and the sound of one tree falling
reverberates like bells and bells and belltowers.

VII. The Underground

Water slides under the rock
    like wine past a dry man's teeth.
A bite out of the heart of stone
    is filled with bats chittering
Tales of rotten fruit and fragrant bones.

Crevices are full of bugs crawling
    the damp and the stone.
The legs feel like feathers,
    cockroach legs, long and spiny,
Delicately rubbing over your ear.

Beetles and larvae crawl
    over your hair except when they weigh
A strand down to dangle before
    your face, multifaceted eyes
Glinting in front of your nose.

Trails of slime drip from hands
    as you crush bugs with every grunting move.
They whisper trails along your cheek,
    brush the palm of your hand,
Bubbling and boiling around you,

A metallic refracting mass of black
    and brown feathered antennae and pincer legs.
And when the bats swoop to make their meal
    and cracked insects plop into the water
Their bite out of the heart of stone

Is a sodden breath of air and a relief
    and the chittering of bats
As they pluck their fruit from your tangled hair
    is wine to a dry man and as welcome
As fresh spring water sliding out of rock.

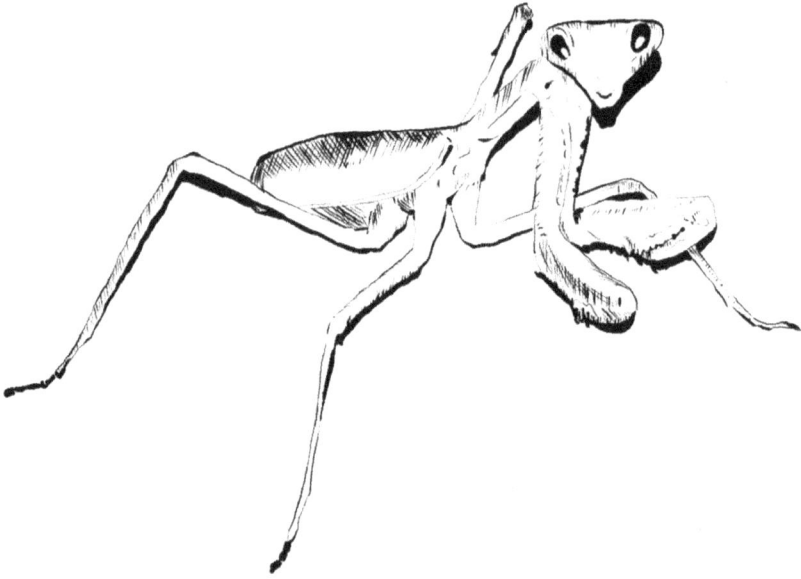

Praying mantis, Rancho Bernardo, California

From Kabul to Kandahar

… The highway between Kabul and Kandahar was supposed to be a success story. Completed in 2003, it has instead become a symbol of all that plagues Afghanistan: insecurity, corruption and the radical Islamic insurgency that feeds off both.—Aryn Baker, Time Magazine, Oct. 31, 2008

"This is my road," Saboor says: a dust
Track gone the long way through the desert rocks.

He drives the bus, two times a week, trusting
Life and face to dirt he smears across

His lips, a beard to baffle Taliban.
He wears mechanic's clothes: a claim the road

Then makes on him, a thieving in the sand,
The way last week the robbers burst and stole

The crates with chickens, goats a-leash, the wealth
That masquerades as dirt itself, the greens.

I ask him, does he fear insurgent's stealth,
The bark of guns, the bullet's code, the dream,

When east Sarobi's tea shops dish fruit cold and sweet,
Pomegranates, porcelain plates, nuts and honey treats,
The scent of lamb in stew, the simmering of the meat—

He shrugs. Stolid, fleet. He says, "This is my road."
It is a dust track where the accent makes the meaning.

❖ Valley in Ancash

I.

We drove through a valley made out of rocks:
A soup bowl filled with pebbles and boulders.
I was retching with the altitude and staring,
nose squashed to the glass, at the few trees whose
spiky brown tops poked above the avalanche.
You said, "There was a town here once, until '71
when the earthquake came. Now all that's left is rocks
and the cemetery, on that rise there, with the trees."
Oh, the road came over the town square
and past the school and flew heavily, paving
bearing down on the beds and the lunch tables
of the people in the stone. And I swooped
with the buildings, up and down, glaring at the gash
in the mountain that made the smell of decay
in my mouth and made me lurch to the window until
you stopped the car and I lost my dinner, over
the graves of the people in the valley, until in stillness,
I stood shuddering, gulping in the high, frigid air.

II.

There are all those people dead and buried in their graves,
all those people that live killing and are killed by uniforms
with men inside, machine guns, hatchets, university professors.
They have the mountains for their tombstone, every rock,
and each one has an oil-covered hand, a political tract,
an unmarked bundle of ragged clothes under it.
In the middle of the night they all get up and dance
a solemn dance around the burned the broken
the still barely standing palm trees that poke above
the burial dirt. The hands have cracked fingernails
and hangnails filled with sting. The papers
flutter and fool around the wind. The trees stand and stand
solemn as guards, stand over all the little kids
who were in the middle of math. They find these
mass graves each day, no names attached on toes,
no dental addresses to carry caskets to.
And I cannot point any fingers, for the world is full of rocks,
full of rocks, of stones, of boulders, and rocks, and stones
are thrown.

III.

There was a huge boulder along the road.
It stood like the mineral answer to the trees
barely visible across the scrabbled sun-choked
valley. There was no graffiti. There were no leaves

caught in its crevices. There was no moss.
It did not roll. There was only the faint scent
of mountain air, of the mountain looming gross
and unmanageable wherever people went.

IV.

I swore I would come to that valley again.
But I feel ashamed to say I have had no dreams.
Let the mountain come to me, so I can
eat the wind, hug the snow-blessed tip, and fall
the thousand miles down to pillow my head
with its mouth full of long-life bile, rest my head
on a softer bed than grass can offer, rest my mind.
I will be the foundation stone of valleys.
Let my back be a swooping road.

❖ Modus ponens

These days, when evil's gene is sequenced, and one percent
Of our species damned, one wonders how the fate
Of empires hinged on changes small as earlobe's bend
Or shape of brow, but was accounted divine punishment.

If this, then that, and therefore so, logicians say.
But erudition falters, premises are false,
And gene expression governs evil RNA,
Which may or may not manifest the Devil's pulse.

Perhaps religion is the gap that Gödel saw,
The faith in something more than systems can contain;
Like Russell's faith, like Whitehead's faith, the futile thought
That logic renders all itself to logic plain.

So all faith hides the knowing; knowing hides some faith.
We speak of evil: don't we mean more than we know?
We mean incomprehensible, Occam's razor failing us,
And Hilbert's second problem writ upon our souls.

Have mercy, then, upon the one percent, who know
Not what they know, three chromosomes from Heaven's glow.

Apples

In Latin, the words for "apple" and for "evil" are similar in the singular (malus—apple, malum—evil) and identical in the plural (mala).—Wikipedia

This apple from Tajikistan gave birth to all the fruit:
The red ones, gold ones, tart ones, green and russet hues.

Each branch was mated to a branch carried over miles
And honeybees deployed in ranks to stoke the woody fires.

The names themselves are everywheres: from Fuji to Orléans,
Grannies, Coxes, McIntoshes and countless other brands,

Which carry in each half-cut star and in their very style
The memory of Kazakh slopes where first they grew in wild.

The blossoms spread, pink and pale verging on the blue,
Until we had the legends: the gold ones Hera grew;

The one that Eris tossed to Paris, causing wars in Troy;
Immortal orchards grown in eddas, Idun's deathless joy;

A snow white princess poisoned; Atalanta's race;
Johnny and all those orchards over which he traipsed;

The tree of knowledge, good and evil, our original sin.
This is quite a burden for fruit to bear within.

We have made the apple ours, and on it grafted history,
And yet the breed runs on, profusions to a tree,

This fruit humanity *resents*, but loves and needs.
Every apple carries still inside those bitter seeds.

Driveways

Under blacktop, dirt and dusty gravel
Struggle with grass breaking the surface.
Entombed squirrel bones pushed by worms travel
Lengthy loam inches beneath silky turf.

This empty mansion, curtained by leaves,
Huge with decay of Duesenbergs
Dead in the garage, vacuous over the scene.
Each day the hinged gates screech twelve unheard.

Until that sly squirrel ventures forth, the latest
In his line to dare the open road, creeping over
Encrypted paths of life beneath, inching towards fate—
Until he's caught by the maw of earth, swallowed.

The dirt and dusty gravel greet the bushy-tail they got:
And then commence exploring his motives, soul, and rot.

Peace

Peace shouldn't be quiet, clouds soft and pliant,
A mellow sky scene in blue.
Peace should be blaring, a jazz band past caring,
A squabble of children and you.
The clangor of pots, your eyes full of spots,
Buttercups growing in dew.
Peace is invention, it's sustained attention,
It's chemistry going kaboom.
It's racing of go karts and artichoke hearts
And farming in Kalamazoo.

It's silence as well, but the silence of bells
The moment they still for a few;
An aftershock sound that echoes around
And gives way to rush and to hue.
It's not smug inertia, safe from what hurts ya;
Pain is what gives us the glue.
It's temperate intemperance, all quantum events,
Mosquitoes buzzing canoes.
A whole raucous party, that's peace's priority:
Space to be scattered and true.

London Squall

Outside a café, London, Aug 2014

London squall, Islington gusts,
Wash the Barbican clean.
Tidy households in tiny flats
Open windows, let out cats
As raindrops stop and shatter
And rental bikes go clattering
Down Clerkenwell streets.

Puddles, unavoidable mess,
Are temporary consequence.
Each lost leaf in King's Square
Is labeled where it fell.
London squall and Islington gusts
May discomfit, yes. But we will not
Permit them to disrupt.

Feather fallen in King's Square, London

Afternoon Joggers

The way they run, struggling against invisible wind,
Great gusts in their chests buffeting them
Like hurricaned pines.

These flagellates billow out each afternoon,
Tilt up slopes I cannot see, at windmills I will not.
They sigh in each night.

This is their duty to themselves, their dream
Of spasms and joints and jolt, their Sisyphean journey
From wind sprints to wind sprites.

❖ Watching a Play

From afar, the patchwork paisleys, tights
and robes, gaudy gowns
a glitter, the ladies

all a carnival, a sumptuous play, riches
on display until full light
hits her full force and then we see

the sawdust backgrounds, painted bright
to eye fool eyefulls, add horizons,
set the stages

gap between surreal, unreal, and real
and really, do they know
the way they fool us themselves?

and then the way the light hits
their saddened eyes
the lacework lashes

such pride in paisley promises
stony pride
in teetering at proscenium's gap

✤ Life Before Light

At night without a lamp, the trees are ghosts;
They loom, they lurk, they fractally recurse.

In depths of shadows howls move, the wolves
Of fear, the snakes of scare, the crows of death.

Come six, the day abed. Come eight, the dark.
And with it, gods: Unknown, Unshaped, Unseen.

What glory dawn has been and is no more!
The restoration of the world we lost.

A scant few decades past this was the world:
A dance of flame to keep the night apart.

And now, our lamps cast pools, candesce, penumb.
The dark is where we hide, where once it hid.

Horizons fade. Our blindness lost, we lose
The splash of Milky Way across the sky.

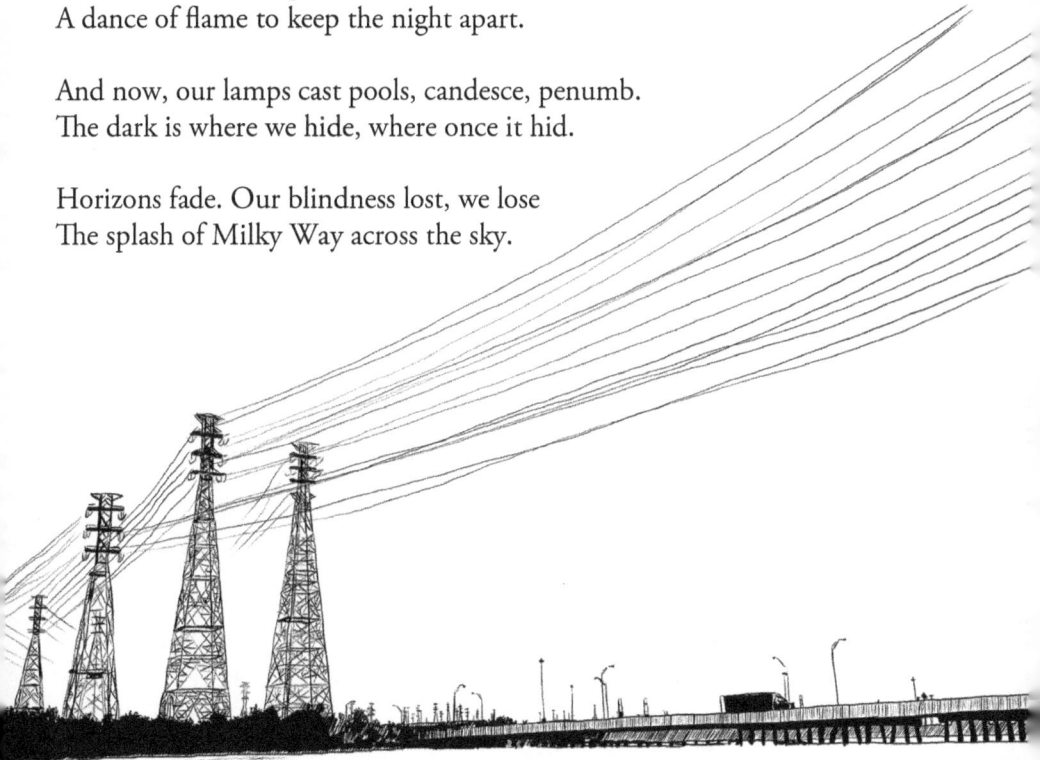

Power lines, Jacksonville, Florida

Eves

Eves are potential: the pendulum at its farthest swing,
The wave as it curls, the indrawn breath, lowered lashes.
They accrete importance, become more the thing than the thing,
Surrounded by lights, by costumes, icons, belled sashes.

The days themselves are rushes, crashes, madness,
The ebb and flow of family, feasts, and fastness.

But eves—eves are frozen, out of time, still and somehow sad—
An endless moment of anticipation you had, but never have.

48

A number shy of fifty, count short of a century's half.
An age where half the time remaining is decline.
A span of time not quite tomorrow, a batch of hours
Piled past a rising sun and past a moonlit night.
The gap of time to find a killer before he's off scot free;
The span of time for ecstasy to filter through a brain.
"A day or two," the time we cite when something needs
Some getting over, the "she'll be better in" refrain.
Anticipation's simplest metric. The continental States.
The year of Paul of Tarsus' mission, when singing
Visions Damascened his eyes. Two even pair of dozens,
A pile of potential chickens, a deck without the kings.
All numbers have their secrets; odd or even, prime or strange.
All figures have their seasons, and all periods have a range.

✤ Circadian

If time is ticking and we tick off time
Then we must be madly ticking, clicking off time
In little hash marks like wrinkles, dimples,
Divots and dashes across ourselves and our minds.

If time is marching and we march through time
Then it must be March, and we push deep into time
With Savings of Daylight and diurnal/nocturnal
Shiftings of time's defining in mind.

But if time is sleeping and we sleepwalk through time
Then we must be dreaming dozing dream logic in time
Just to awaken when clocks clack and cackle

Their shocking take on the time of our minds.
If time is precious, then I must prize this time
Spent sleeping, an hour lost just… in time.

The Clock Before Falling Asleep

It's not tick tock. More like a
Tack chalk tick chalk take chalk talk chalk,
A song without sibilants whinging its way
Around the vowels, never settling, circling back.

As you sleep it falls into white noise,
Just chalk chock shock sock until every moment
Blurs its way into the melting dream.
Marking moments that move sideways,

Perpendicular to seeing, the sibilants easing
Their way into the susurration of sleep.
Each six degrees of movement, each sharp tick
The peak signal in a rush of static.

What is a clock? A simplistic rhythm, like chalk itself,
Nothing more than a rubbing on the face of time.

Herbie Hancock on a Headache

The thundundering of the duhduhdurums,
The lashing of the cymbal crasharashing.
Piano diddledaddle flatting fives and nattering,
The bass boom thrumming thump thrump on.

Play the drum head, pound that skin,
Send jolts of timbre dazzle down my spine.
Blow my mind, bounce the skull, a countercoup,
Ivories xylophoning tickles in a line.

But the music, music, music ocean sloshing close,
Washing-whipping, whirl-a-looping, a vortex
Vast and varied with snatches of a song;
In fugue I fade before too long, the scribbled charts

Rocking me to sleep, eleventh for a pillow,
The tang and ride a blanket muffling me to dark.

Departures

Life is made of departures:
The passage from the dark
The moment of weaning's sharp
Longing, frantic gestures.

Balloons slipping out of hands.
A dog's last stiff-legged sleep.
Kisses in a closet, the deep
Fear there, the moments grand.

The move from maiden name
And the way she feels once
Delivered. A man who hunts
Regrets, and finds just blame.

Life is made of departures
And occasional desperate returns

The Miraflores Lighthouse, Lima, Peru

Lullabye: Waking Dream

Sing yourself to sleep, my sweet, and settle down the moon.
The countries found beyond the night are rich with tourist sites:
Plot your dreaming carefully, and do not wake too soon.

As sirens call you now and bye, a subtle lull, a croon,
Take big strides through vasty lands purpled with delight.
Sing yourself to sleep, my sweet, and settle down the moon.

Do not fear oblivion's near, that sleep is like a tomb;
You stand on precipices made of cotton candy light!
Plot your dreaming carefully, and do not wake too soon.

There will be sweet wine, warm food, and melodies of June,
The arias of April and the meters of the night.
Sing yourself to sleep, my sweet, and settle down the moon.

To dream is not a punishment. To live is not a doom.
The two entwine within your eyes, the eyes you kept so bright.
Plot your dreaming carefully, and do not wake too soon.

And now you're older, old, and old for dreaming's final rites,
Know the paths you trod remain, in darkness as in life;
Sing yourself to sleep, my sweet, and settle down the moon.
Plot your dreaming carefully, and do not wake too soon.

Working Late

Birds stud the late night lot, move like skipping stones.
The bi-illumined trees huddle parking lights, dance
the empty parking spots, waltzing without parts, alone.

We click, we clack, we open, close, liquid crystal glows.
We do the work we love, the love is like a trance.
Birds stud the late night lot, move like skipping stones.

The stairwell window's open. The breeze is cold and stone.
The smokers huddled there and overlooked by chance
the empty parking spots, waltzing without parts, alone.

Last lights are off. Hallway's dim. The music of alarm tones.
We promised not to stay so late, not to see sunset's hands
scatter birds, the late night lot, moved like skipping stones.

But it works. Assembly is complete. The work, it can be shown,
a tiny victory, a dinner lost, traded for the midnight glance
at empty parking, spouse waltzing without partners, lonely.

We move like skipping stones through dances grown
to dreams; we work for dreams we only hope enhance.
We stud the late night lot. We move like skipping stones
past empty parking spots. We waltz our parts, and do not dance alone.

Earthquakes and Oceans

The land is under the sky
And the ocean is under the sky
But the land is also under the ocean.
Beneath, the grumbling tectonic heave
Of molten earth, breaking angry creases
Open in what is really a very thin skin,
Reminds us of the narrow shell
Covering all great heats. It is like that,
When I see her, and I feel the cracks
Open, tremors crazing, until to say
Anything is a quiet earthquake in me.
I could break—
But the sky is over the land
And the sky is over the ocean,
The sky everlasting.
The ocean is dammed within,
Ready to flow and beat its waves
Against any shore accessible,
Full and patient,
Waiting.

Anywhere

You smell like your body,
You feel like your skin.
I would know you anywhere.
I would know you any when.

You sound like your voice.
You walk like your pace.
You touch like your heart.
You smile like your face.

You shout like your anger,
Forgive like your pain.
I would know you anywhere.
I would know you any when.

You comfort like sorrow.
You give like you're giving.
I would know you in a crowd
By the sound of your breathing.

You see like your eyes.
And then you see me, and then
I would know you anywhere.
I would know you any when.

Life and Love

Life is not sacred. It is precious.
There is a difference: the world
Cheerfully slaughters the innocent,
The accidental, the promising.

Each blade of grass is life;
Each microbe on a grain of sand.
Each blastocyst, each parasite,
Each recombinant acid bit.

Each set of neurons firing,
Each varied, vertiginous
Set of senses, inchoate reactions,
Pathways burned through myelin.

Thin-veined leaves uncurling spring,
Each water-cupping hydrozoa,
Human fingers questing for a touch—
Not special. Just marvelous.

Mourning, we mourn the instance.
Not webs of cells, mitochondria,
The symbiotes that link
The web of life from us to them.

We mourn instead intangibles:
The days not gone by, completing
Each other's thoughts, the dance
Of neurons mirroring.

These are intentions, not blind
Questing, not propagation
Creeping its way across the blank.
These are bounds beyond biology.

There is a difference: the world
Knows life as tumbles of succession,
Accidental promising. But love—ah,
Love is not precious. It is sacred.

❖ Caledonian Creation Myth

It begins, a courtship
Like others, earth and wave
Meeting on the strands
And sand, a wet periphery, an
Intersection. He laps at her
Shores, and she erodes until
In time the tide of moons,
Of fancies, of chocolates and
Flowers, of all the mechanisms of the heart,
Bring them to lick salt from each other—
Salt of earth, of sea—until
They merge in the movement of the ocean.
From this, a life is born.
It is like this everywhere—
Everywhere it is like this.

I Saw and Heard

A tethered girl with a guitar, restringing
On a park bench, clothes and voice wringing
Wrinkles from a rag. She twitched her head,
A nervous finch, her bones aslide, fluid
Bumps beneath her drum-tight skin, a flock
Of birds enclosed by brittle flesh, a-cracking,
And cracking only when she sang.

                                        I feel
A minor need to make her something real:
To steal aloft the eagles trapped within,
To cut them free from helpless hampering skin,
Take hold of jesses, loose them in a spasm,
To watch the music soar past sky and chasm.

But "real" lies in beholder's hearts, and "real"
Is not lived day to day—is just a tale
Told to children full of fancy dreams,
Who picture avian souls and eagle's screams.

The whole short scene was just her playing.
She'd sung some words before, I'd say,
Will sing again, will strive, earn cash, survive,
And lyrics do not modulate our lives.

But where is the poem in that?

Seagull, Santa Monica Pier

Logomachia

Imagine this library here before you
If every cover fell away and melted
Into puddles of shiny water. If the thread
Of binding serpentined along the floors
And twined around the legs of chairs.
I finger all these spines of me,
And think of a body of leaves
Rustling to patterns I can't follow.
How glorious to see pages that have never met
Come face to face and taste each other's ink.
How awful to face the mass of sodden pulp
And be unable to enter at any point.

This has already happened. It has always happened.

✤ [citation needed]

The absence of evidence ain't evidence,
Every evidence's evidently incomplete;
Each fact is wrapped in negative space
And stands on wobbly feet.

The nature of truth is always interpreted,
As footnotes assume and sum up and complete;
Each fact is attached to big old philosophies.
Sophistry's got quite a beat.

The final of science is constant revision;
The personal touch is political need;
The NPOV is drawn from bad sources
And taint runs from crown down to seed.

Opinions are crowding around us,
We're armies each time we believe.
We lead crusades on simple so-says,
Rhetoric sharpened to bleed.

Nothing is simple and true.
Nothing is filling the feed.
Nothing is between the atoms.
Nothing is what we tweet.

Yet I find in the gaps and the space the mellifluous cadence; rough dance
Of ideas, the provisional truth, the occasion to meet with some, all
-ternate minds. Sometimes citation needed is space to connect;
Apprehension can be system-wide, even if all footnotes lie.

So link away. Your rabbit holes don't daunt.
Follow the rhizome back to its roots.
You won't find an answer, just more mechanics,
But its dynamics are an answer that suits.

❖ The State of Poetry

"I wrote a poem for you."
She smiled, that half-smile,
Moue waiting in the wings.
Once it was unfolded, she
Passed it to her friend, who,
Furrowed, said, "Not my thing,
But I am sure it's very nice."

"I wrote a poem for you."
He froze, sudden trapped fear
Shaping muscles. Once read,
Twice the wrong questions
Danced in his eyes.

I wrote a poem for you.
Do poems always mean
Something other than they say?

Spiderwebs in Dew

Some things can only be seen
Spattered, smeared, beaded
By accretions. Rendered visibly
Useless, an easy target for avoidance.
Magnificent cathedrals honored
Only in their ruin, awaiting
The touch of attenuating sun
Gentle enough to cleanse them
To their clinging state of absence.

Some things are awesome
Only with invisibility:
The card sharp's flick,
Magician's trick, effortless
Soaring of a voice. Others
Revel in acceptance: arm-thick
Cabling suspending bridges,
The shuddering grunt of muscle;
Admiring machinery and not result.

By dusk the spider hovers
Magical, target center in
Invisible bullseyes.
By dawn the bullseye shines
But the magic show is over.
The age-old question looms,
Which is the greater work?
The cathedral or the architect?
The trickster or the trick?

✤ Diminuendo

Suppose you plucked a string,
And made the silly sound thing
Play a tune and learn to sing.

Suppose you pulled it strong,
Yanked the note loud and long
Until it barely knew its song.

Suppose you made it snap and growl,
Teased it till it spat and howled,
Coaxed it as it sank and cowled.

Would you think you had the credit?
It was the string that sounded—bled it.
It wasn't you who said it.

We shape the sound through pressure
And treat the music as our leisure
And let it flow through its own measures.

We rarely see it stand alone,
The music without a player's tone,
The dots and dashes fully grown.

Suppose you plucked a string,
Suppose you pulled it strong,
Suppose you made it snap and growl,
Dots and dashes fully grown.
Would you think you had the credit?
It was the string that shone.
Or was it you that said it?

SUNDAY POEMS

Guitar headstock

❖ 24 Views of Mt. Fuji

Hokusai the gremlin's job is very simple:
each hour of the day
           he scrambles
across Linotype and makes
                "bloody sunlight
shrouding the barn"
           into "dappled apples
of light made the barn an orchard."

He flips through floppy disks and demagnetizes
"her bloated corpse, boiling with decay,"
                  to "her body,
one breath past sleep."
           He pauses at "a stink
like grade school frogs and formaldehyde"
but shrugs and leaves it at
             "the stink of a fresh
broken bottle of perfume"
           He stares at
"my mistress' eyes" and smiles.

This is not a children's book. Look at the artistry:

The careful gradual introduction
               of perspective,
the influence of the few Western paintings he's seen.

The gigantic somber glow of Red Fuji climbs off
the page,
        claims its own standing,
                "a demonic
shape cast from iron, not yet cooled,"
               the view past
the boatmakers, the men building the houses, the view
up the river,
        under the bridge, "a mountain reduced
to an icon, snow dabbed on its tip like the brush strokes"
"of a feather dipped in blood," "serene in the distance
and as unreachable as" "the slope we walk on, feet slapping"

the gremlin smiles and Fuji grows around us,
Hokusai
how well you have wrought

⚜ Nude Descending a Staircase
(the nude's monologue)

This is a day when I can't remember my name, dear
   (I do not dress with no name)
I am unpatterned and you did it to me
I suppose you feel happy wherever it is you've gone
         (I took that earring and bent it and twisted it
           it broke)
        nyaaaah
        I'm still trying to get off these stairs, where I walk and walk and walk
        an orange square
          a blue rectangle
These steps: my calves are aching like compressed steel
       my heels are nails driven
       the case hammers my spine
       I am unmade, dear
       an orange rectangle
         a blue square
Arms in light   head in shadow
   striped by blows of window & sun
      a bright surface
       a smooth plane
help me you bastard
       I cannot stop moving
       (my clockwork is sprung)
    All I expected was a chance to fit in   to be a figure
like other figures I've seen   a figure with a place to stand
     not the kitchen making dinners for you
    not the mother with a baby and another on the way
just me   just someone with a name and a house with white walls
     I found her earring in our bedspread   (that's how I know)
      an orange square
       a bent angle
good riddance to you and to her too
        sorry I can't wear those strapless things
   black doesn't suit me, velvet itches, satin slides
but I really want to be held right now and you can't do it anymore
(I might even try if you'd come find me)
         all my peaces waiting to be picked up

put   me   in   a   box,   a   perfect
right   angled   box,   with   sturdy
sides   and   rigid   corners,   a box,
then   I'll   know   what   to   do, dear,
in a lovely box I'll know what to do
in a box   in a   box   in a box in a
please   write   on   the   side

I can't tell who I am without your label

✤ Guernica

A separation of pigments: my point of view is not where I look

I can only filter events through newsprint
Picasso's grey immanence pervades and defines

Where is the gradual nervousness?
The regime pilot's eye as he drops the bomb?
Staring at the elongated frame that focusses
straining at the edge of canvas:

The hoarse of a scream
is dirt driven deep under fingernails
The scream of a horse is scrabbling
Guernica:
how terrifying to be told where to think
how to think
the shape of thinking
how peaceful

✤ Paradise Shark

The best sort of shark,
Chasing longfins too large
To mouth, graceful grey,
Paint fleck fins, a lofty
Catfish, small, not big
Enough to eat but proud
Of hunting, his name
An attitude, a look, and
All the teeth he needs.

Since the Zombies Came

Since the zombies came, you can't get decent sushi;
Zombie sludge, it spoils fish like nothing doing.
And all the second hand stores, they had to close up shop…
Stains just don't wash out the way they used to, do they?

Stuff that's better—well, the horror flicks, of course. Duh.
Extras just show up. And don't need paid, or credit.
Watch at home, though! Darkened cineplexes…
Real bad news. Though crowds are thinner at the malls now.

'Sides, the zombies, mostly peaceful, right? Like yoga,
Tai chi, meditation, all that shit. OMMMM, then
Nom nom BRAAAIIIINS. They mostly stand and stare in corners
Seeing into places we cannot with jelly

Eyes and dreaming of the sushi and the clothes, the
Pay and credit, ordinary hungers (BRAAAIIIINS), good
Posture, faces still intact, more moods than one… sad.
Pity them; resent them, for the sushi's sake.

Worse? It could be worse, sure. Aliens are worse, right?
Zombies get you, BRAAAIIIINS, you're dead, undead, whatever.
Aliens, you live on screaming, tentacles in
Awkward places, slaved. I'd rather eat my friends, thanks.

❖ Soul Food

If we are what we eat then dogs are kibble,
All bounding grains and some
Substantial portion of lamb.
And us? Walking past a park we are all

Gangly asparagus and sly cabbage,
Chicken more often than we'd like,
All too often greasy fingered from fast
Eatings, while time takes away time.

Society ladies folded and folded over
Canapés, some revealing dustbin leftovers
And a sandpaper heart, others housing
A surprise of flavor within complexity.

Powerful men made of the juices
Of dried up things, raisins and plums,
Often sniffed and judged wanting, with
All the taste in the bouquet.

Working men, beefy and blood red
Hearty from the day and from the dirt,
With a dash of potatoes behind their ears
And a dash of hops to keep their heads up.

Last, a surprise, the girls from both coasts,
Willowy to haggard, caught in their seasons,
Rose and primrose, orchid, dandelion,
Haughty, wondrous gaudy, tasteless flowers.

Out of Water

Today she walks on solid ground, but once

The world was water, every touch a wave,
And all her friends were mermaids, shelled and sleek.
The house that kept her safe, the walls of kelp,
The bed of coral-stone, were just a current
Lashed around a dock, with fish asleep
In all the reef's crannies. The sharks stood guard
And crabs trickled like mercury on glass.

Today she walks on solid ground, where none
Can fly, where there is no clear ceiling on,
Where she is told she ought to try to climb
Beyond the blue. She digs her toes in deep,
Kneels, clutches hands of dirt and pebbles, and
In her liquid voice, mourns the oceans passed
Beyond her eyes. And all is well with us

To know she sees with us again; it scares
Us deep to know someone who drinks where no-one dares.

SUNDAY POEMS

Swans in Lake Zurich, Switzerland

The Dragons and Me

The dragons and me, well, we used to argue.
We had these fantastically frightening rows.
I tell you this to explain, not alarm you.

They wore fedoras and chomped old cigars,
And liked wearing ponchos on great horny toes.
But really, they loved most going too far.

They'd flame with no motive, follow the stars through,
They'd hoard things for reasons only they know.
I tell you this to explain, not alarm you.

Oh, after, sure, apologies offered, eyes all a-sorrow.
It was just in their nature to carry on so.
How the dragons and me used to argue, you know!

The day they departed, they kept secrets from me:
The reasons they left, the ebb and the flow.
I tell you this to explain, can't you see?

As they booked one-way passage from Earth on to Mars,
I wanted to travel, go too far, where they go.
But no, they said, no, you're not made for the stars.

I still love far countries, though for now I am for you.
You understand now, the ebb? Hold me close.
The dragons and me, well, we used to argue,
And I still can't quite tell how far I can go.

❖ Goety

When summoning demons, a grammar's required,
A grimoire, a ponderous tome of desires.
Arsenic, candlelight, horsehair and fires,
Upside-down symbols and unholy choirs.

The cerements, synapses, salts and surprises,
The deal signed in blood with fine printed clauses,
The pyxes, ciboria, the desecrate losses,
Impertinent heresies, thumbing of noses.

The grammar, the numbers, the deep structured cadence
All echo grimmer and deeper acquaintance:
That grammar and glamour were once the same radix,
A fear of high language confusing plebeians.

For weavers of spellwords were once naught but poets,
Summoning demons though they might not know it:
When conjuring shades or religions, their souls writ
Political speeches and potboiler spirits.

By these lights, each writerly pen is a chalice
Filled with the ink of heretical magic.
Our mistrust of language runs deep through our practice,
For Words were the mystery, chanting and tragic.

✤ The Pangrammatic Fox

The quick brown fox, they claim, jumped the lazy dogs, over and more, forever
cycling mad her quota'd alphabets, leveling Zipf, an indexed joker wild.

Unlucky vixen, pangram beast, spending q's and hoarding j's, the thrifty ditzy wench!
Why futz phonemes fro and to, when flow twixt verbs and jokes, the cogs of status quo,

Delights us so? Books bursting free the japes, glyphs, queries, catalexis, zeugmas woven
From quotidian words to dazzle, vex, illumine, pry, and beckon us! Why judge letters equal?

Math must be seizing Reynard's mind, values coffling waxing jabber, equations poking
'Til nothing's left except a pangrammatic sieve, quibbling z's and k's; hortatory, just and swift.

✤ Flicker

People worked hard for their reading once, and perhaps valued it the more:
The wind battering their pages as they sought light away from musty houses,
The flick flick flicker of the candle oscillating letters in the night.

People worked hard for their writing once, the flick flick flicker of their pens
Scratching inkspot nibs and spatters, forming letters finely crafted almost
    accidental,
Their minds battering their pages as they sought light away from musty
    houses.

People valued this knowledge once, the knowledge of not being in the cult of
    ignorance,
The ignorance of knowledge of working hard for their books, the knowledge
Of ignorance flick flick flickering away the lights of musty houses

In favor of the howl of the wind, and the winding of the sheets of time
    battering
Down the oscillation of human hearts and minds. These were such small
    battles:
The flicking of eyes across candle-lit pages, the pages themselves, against the
    night.

Preserved; saved; these flickers, musty now themselves, bound and spined and
    sold
By bucketfuls and carts in bookstores proud to carry old soldiers termed as
    "used."
I worked hard for my reading once, and wrote, and now all is mere commerce
    and gratuity.

❖ The Age of the Computer Poem

It began when Apple let loose
With their copyright-defending Truth™:

Embedding bad rhymes within coding,
Chmodding the zeitgeist, foreboding,
And opening heretofore shut doors
That scare us deep in multicores:
Whe'er pentameter's big or little endian,
And runs on platforms Intellian…
Where emulators handle sestinas
Composed on Javascript machine-as
And sonnets are source if Petrarchan
But GIGO rhymed with ABAB markin's.

This was all merely the very first move;
Dell trumped them with their try to prove
They were better at poetic pennings
With ads shaped as Old English kennings.
Furor over rewording of "IM" erupted
As Utah felt youths were being corrupted.
IBM made their market share worse
Writing manuals in rigid blank verse,
And little market acceptance
Went to Linux encoded as jazz dance.

Soon no code could be written sans zeugmas.
MSCE's were swapped for what, truth was,
Formerly useless higher-ed vellum,
A certification quite antebellum:
MFA's, now granted by tech schools
Scared to be left-in-the-dust fools,
Reduced to hacking "the dozens"
While envying the tech of their cousins
In the English department, who all gloated:
Content in a land
    where all coding
        was now double-coded.

⟡ Network Optimization

Packet size, packet size, info little lump,
    This coded, that coded, TCP'ed and dumped.
Piling into buffers, stacking up the K,
    Header bettered, ack lettered, MD5ed in clumps.

Metrics march, events arch, tallying the toil,
    Adding tag, another tag, to running tallies coiled.
Graphs and means and peak machines,
    Lists linked, map inserts, cauldron bubble boil.

Pixel bobble, bubble wobble, choke the data down!
    Another bar, three sorts so far, infoviz may drown.
Watch the python nybble tail, log files swell the mail.
    Second sampled average trampled, occasioning a frown.

The buckets pause, optimal lost; packets stay for free.
    Bottom line, too many lumps of data with your tea.
Machinery in motion, gears a-clank and potent,
    Guzzle not, and thirst not, you cramp your buffered belly.

Packet size, packet size, info little lump,
    This coded, that recoded, TCP'ed and dumped.

✤ Ode to Code: A Geek Poem

Just think:
The twine of sine
and cosine, twang of tangents,
tangles of angles and twirls of tris,
the way each curve is wavelength,
like a sound is wavelength, light is
wavelength. A four forty's tone
is blue, its hertz a wiggle,
wobble, flow from
high to low, a
nanometer's
drunken walk
the shade of skies.

Perhaps by this was Schumann
driven mad; the way the math invades,
pervades, like A four forty in his ear
for years: a cosmic radio of audio
uncaused by any known thing.
Oh, the song was blue,
but blues were
something
Schumann
never heard.
Or always did.
Or thought he always did.

The azimuth, horizon, incidence;
The cadence, coda, recapitulation.
These are all the whirlwind tang of life:
From helices in mitochondria to lacy
fractal leaves to strings vibrating
quarks, and time we see
cross-sectioned.
Here we
have the arc
of it, the seconds. Mark.

And now, we twist our code
in loops, recurse in tighter spirals, flow
through chains of consequence—input
output GIGO FILO—at play with toys
that mimic magic, reify and
retro-fy, a Bezier here,
vector there,
a wave
of bosses, twirl
Of blues, a count of lives, all binary.

Signs, sines, sprites, twines, tangents, tunes, time. In rhyme.

❖ The BASICs of life

10 Dimension all your variables, figure out their sides.
20 Remark, perhaps, on how data twirls across divides.
30 Print a hello world, as if the world could not read cursive;
40 Go to thirty, looped but still printed, not recursive.
50 For once you have some code that doesn't do much else,
60 Next you'll want to make it special, of yourself.
70 Data will be read, perhaps, or Fibonacci spun,
80 While you tally figures until the job is done.
90 Poke a byte, peek a bit, nybble 'til you're through,
100 End with too few memories, dimensions still unused.

Puzzle Poetry

A poem where the lines cannot add up.
Where verbs and nouns are hidden; you must find.
Where rhymes are slanted indiscriminate,
And rhythms pop and prattle out of tune.

It's not like it's all done on purpose—no!
We try to make the words convey the most
We can, and sometimes they convey too much.
They overflow, and simple matters mud.

In part, the puzzle lies with us, who craft
The lines and lessons into sonnets. We
Are piecing syllables and skeletons.
We try to make the lines add up to truth.

We fail, and sense is lost cacophonous and ground.
We reach mellifluous success, and then it's lost in color, and in sound.

When is a Rhyme a Rhyme?

When is a rhyme a rhyme? A pair of words
Vibrating twain and twin, a homonym
A scanty, scarcely fraction time, a blur
Of vowels assonancing on a whim...
Half verb, the penult, higher ante, quill
That sometimes speaks in halves and sometimes sprung,
And in the clumsy piling on of syll,
The ables and alliterate undone.
Is all it is the music? Nothing else
Applies? The quatrain's break, the plosive sound,
The prayer on the couplet's open verse?
The sense of it, the consonance profound?
The algorithm elegant, the twinning still sublime,
Is it still a poem, if we forget to rhyme?

✤ If you…

…Push through the keys on a piano, what's on the other side?
Not wires and hammers; not wood, but desires.
An echoing chamber of fires and lovers and lies.

…Bite through the skin of an orange, what's on the other side?
Not citrus but summer, both light and burnt umber,
A country far distant all tart and remembered and bright.

…Look through the slits of an outlet, what's on the other side?
Not six thousand currents pulsing reverberant,
But magic brought low, in harness instead of in sky.

…Stretch through the screens all around you, what's on the other side?
We reach for each other through bytes and through phosphor,
Past Borges' big library, at play in the forms we provide.

We never think shells are the essence; we crack without asking why.

For Every Fiddle Found

For every fiddle found in an old pawn shop
There is a gypsy less, with music torn away.
I brushed at the smeary dust and tapped
The wood, to hear the hollowness. Atop
The counter I also saw a hoary dredel,
A metal top, a magic deck of cards, and, trapped
In amber, a fly at table on some ancient tree.

The owner sat like crumpled paper on his stool
And snored the day along, foot swinging slow,
In counterpoint to the Swiss pendulum behind.
The shop sold many objects but no tools,
Except the violin, an instrument I didn't know.
The dust encased the place and to my mind
Held it still. I turned to go, the tuneful gypsy

Banished from my mind, shoulders aching to build
Before they tired from the weight of centuries
And went still, motionless like stone, killed
By whistling dirges in the sun.

Outside the wind was fresh, the road was long,
And there were naughty kids to capture,
Dancers to seduce with living songs.

SUNDAY POEMS

Notes

Why It Is Hard. "In science one tries to tell people, in such a way as to be understood by everyone, something that no one ever knew before. But in poetry, it's the exact opposite."–Paul Dirac. Thanks to blog commenter Rich Bryant for the quote.

Pistachio. After the poem "Why It Is Hard," a blog commenter named Amaranthar challenged me with "Ok, a challenge. Next Sunday do a poem on Ice Cream Cones, and do it without any insinuations of death, love, or nature." This, of course, is pretty impossible (*no* insinuations, at all?) so I wrote this poem, inspired by childhood walks with my maternal grandfather.

Suomi. Suomi is the original name of Finland. This poem is referencing Vappu, the May Day or Walpurgis Night festival in Finland. All the alumni of the universities gather in the park in Helsinki wearing the white tasseled caps they received upon graduation. Needless to say, it can still be quite rainy and cold on May Day in Finland; it's quite far to the north.

Balloon over Rancho Santa Fe, California

The Road to Whimsy. This poem is about walking to the Ghibli Museum in Mitaka, Japan. Studio Ghibli is the animation studio responsible for films such as *My Neighbor Totoro* (whence the cat bus).

We did open doors. There were these little doors in one exhibit, and inside one there was a perfect miniature version of the Studio Ghibli working area.

We did see a butterfly that size. Or moth. Or bat. I am unsure now.

The side roads had green bicycle lanes. And yes, they were bouncy—they felt like the surfacing in playgrounds.

We did see a man with a hawk on his arm. I didn't snap his picture though.

It is true you cannot eat inside the museum. However, the Three Bears exhibit had a giant table where kids were spilling beans from giant bowls with great abandon. Diligent Japanese parents were sweeping them all back up and putting them back in the bowl.

No photos either. But most of the stuff on the walls was unframed—it was just watercolors and pencils, literally tacked up with thumbtacks.

Robots, of course. Especially the one from *Castle in the Sky* that is on the roof. But also many stroboscope-based exhibits of stop-motion animation, vintage stuff from the Victorians, and so on. The flock of sparrows was one such exhibit, with flickering lights making the birds fly around the robot. The spider's web was on the walk there—a truly enormous garden spider.

Doug Church had brought these amazing grapes. I literally never tasted a better grape in my life. But I substituted ice cream for the flavor.

Only really little kids are allowed on the cat bus.

Sometimes a Duck is Just a Duck. "When I see a bird that walks like a duck and swims like a duck and quacks like a duck, I call that bird a duck."– attributed to James Whitcomb Riley. This little trifle came about because there was active debate on the issue of whether using strategy guides and hint books was considered to be cheating at a game. I found people's definitions of what constituted cheating to be highly erratic at best, and the wide array of opinions expressed resulted in this poem.

The Piano Teacher's House. This poem, oddly enough, was born from game level design. Back in the early 1990's I was designing a game area for *LegendMUD* based on exploring a stereotypical 1950s small town. The piano teacher's house was one of the places you could explore.

Davey Flower Becomes a Pterodactyl. My son David (whom we have never called Davey) sometimes played at being a dinosaur. However, we never had hamsters after the kids were born, and never kept goldfish per se; other sorts of fish instead. Oh, and there's no baby Frank, but my dad's name is Francis.

Clouds From Above. I wrote this on a trip in Asia, my head still full of Chinese dragons and the tallest building in the world. As we went through the amazing-looking clouds, I couldn't help but think how cold, wet, and basically depressing they are, even though from the ground we once thought them fluffy and warm and magical. And that led me on a train of thought about how our perspective as humans has changed, over time, and how perhaps, really, *we* are the mythological creatures that assert dominion over nature.

I ended up using Western mythology (Arthurian specifically) because that was the best-known clash of dragons… Tintagel Castle was, in Arthurian legend, where Ygraine was seduced by Uther Pendragon, eventually resulting in baby Arthur. Many novelists have cast this as a battle between a red and a white dragon.

Descending to the Airport at Night. This one's bones came to me on a return flight from up the California coast, seeing the marine layer hovering at the edge of the ocean. It sat tall, far taller than any of the hills or cliffs. It looked a cliff itself, a glacier, maybe The Wall from *Game of Thrones,* overhanging the land. It looked like a shoreline in an inverted world where everything we are was lost in the dark except the little twinkling lights.

Seeing the clouds as an ocean is hardly new, of course, but it stuck with me as we descended. I thought about the liminal perspective a plane affords, an upbringing affords, and recited phrases to myself, trying to commit them to memory before they darted away like nervous fish. It has seen minimal revision from that version, scribbled onto an iPad in the airport parking lot.

If Trees Did Not Stop Growing. We spent some time that day at the park at a Cub Scout event, and I fell asleep on our blanket on the grass, staring up at the maze of intersecting branches, and at the smooth-trunked trees that vaulted to the blue. I was struck by how alike the grasses were, the same shapes and forks and blind reaching for the sun, the way that the water grasses arching over the little stream were hiding tadpoles from my glance, and the way the bigger boughs made the sun dart in and out like flashing flickers on a fish—was something watching us?

It made me think, if trees are just huge grass, then what grows huger still?

Driving to Tainan. Tainan is a city in southern Taiwan.

Lions in Vegas. An ersatz villanelle, written hurriedly amidst the endless noise of casinos. The lions in question do have their bubbly fifty acres within the heart of the MGM Grand. You can walk under them and look at their big plush paws as they sleep on the transparent floor for their six-hour shift, after which they go home to their Vegas home off the Strip, like every other performer there.

A Cherufe Tale. This one resulted from reading Isabel Allende's *Inés of My Soul,* which brought back many memories of hours reading into the stories of the conquistadors. Truly amazing stories, full of gore and ridiculous heroism and unspeakable exploitation and rank stupidity. I had forgotten the story of the conquest of Chile, which didn't really even end until the 1800's. Read on for the summary...

This poem barely skims the surface of a truly crazy narrative. Pedro de Valdivia left his young wife in Spain, but is often accounted one of the few honorable conquistadors. He met Inés de Suarez, who can only be described as a badass, and together with a few Spanish and a lot of natives (mostly from tribes conquered by the Inca) crossed the Atacama Desert in the second expedition to try to colonize what is today called Chile. They founded Santiago, today the capital.

At one point, Inés defended the village by chopping off the heads of seven hostages and riding out in armor. She was married off to one of his captains by viceroyal order, because she and Pedro couldn't be seen to live in sin. She went on to become essentially the founding mother of Chile, and that captain[1] became governor after Valdivia.

De Valdivia had a stable boy who was Mapoche, of the native Chilean Indians. This boy, Lautaro, ran away to become one of the great generals in history, developing countless guerrilla tactics still studied today. The Spanish kept trying to cross into Mapoche territory past the Biobío River. Eventually, Lautaro defeated Valdivia, and the conquistador died in a manner fitting with his thirst for gold: they poured the molten stuff down his throat until he died.

---

[1] Rodrigo de Quiroga.

Although Lautaro died soon after, the wars went on, and on.[2] But that city by the Biobío that Valdivia founded, Concepción, is where Chile declared independence. Ironically, it was an Irish family that did it.

Somehow, it struck me that the old Chilean tales of *cherufes*, or volcano spirits that demand sacrifices, was a decent metaphor for Valdivia's life as a whole; in the poem, he is the sacrifice for the birth of a new country.

All Stories Are Like This. This arose from a pointer in John Crowley's blog to a project entitled "The Whole Five Feet," wherein a writer in New York named Christopher Beha was reading through the five-foot shelf that is the Harvard Classics.[3] Basically, it's a collection put together in the early part of last century of 5 feet of books that could substitute for a liberal education. My house being what it was, as a child, we didn't have this; we instead had the Britannica *Great Books of the Western World*, which is where I first read Jonathan Swift, *Gargantua and Pantagruel*, Plato, and Homer. This would have been when I was ten or eleven.

Most people do not have *Gargantua and Pantagruel* in their home libraries. Indeed, I don't today. The very notion of what makes for an education has shifted significantly. Today, I am told that spelling isn't important to pin down at this developmental stage, so "inventive spelling" is allowed for my children.

The funny thing, of course, is that certain things always recur. We might not have Gargantua himself, though some argue that we have the echoes of the Abbey of Thélème.[4] (Try tracing from that to St Augustine to Aleister Crowley and thence to Satanism, Wicca, and controversies over *Dungeons & Dragons*—it isn't hard).

So when I see a perfectly old-fashioned ghost story mentioned in Beha's post on Pliny,[5] one that would be at home in M. R. James or on *The Twilight Zone,* or even in the hands of the director of a modern Japanese horror film, it prompts some pondering on what exactly survives us, as storytellers or as readers.

Pliny himself wanted to live forever as a great name. He may or may not be making the grade. But then, over the truly long haul, we live on more as echoes than as sounds, more as retellings than as the original story.

---

[2] These are the Arauco Wars, fought off and on from 1536 to 1825.
[3] This project eventually became a book of the same title, which I have not read.
[4] https://en.wikipedia.org/wiki/Fran%C3%A7ois_Rabelais#Th.C3.A9l.C3.A8me
[5] http://thewholefivefeet.typepad.com/the_whole_five_feet/2007/03/volume-9.html

Building the Globe. As the story goes, the owner of the Shoreditch land where The Theatre stood didn't want to renew the lease. This caused problems for Richard and Cuthbert Burbage, because although they had inherited the actual structure from their father James, the owner could and did simply bar them from using the land. And The Theatre was special—the very first theater in London *ever*, for until then plays were played in courtyards of inns. So they got Peter Streete, a master carpenter, to help them; and then the actors themselves crossed the river to sneak in and dismantle the old theater building. Then they sailed the huge oak beams and other pieces across the Thames, and reassembled it under Streete's guidance in a pretty field in Southwark.

No small task, but that's how the structure that we know as The Globe Theatre was born: assembled out of the numbered pieces of another building, smuggled over the water and past an angry landlord's eye. The structure was shaped like an O, with no roof above the standing area where the low-paying groundlings stood to watch. But the stage itself was covered by a small roof, with a sky painted on it, moon, stars, and sun. All told, the structure held several thousand. Some of the columns were painted carefully to trick the eye into seeing marble, but really, it was all flammable wood—which was eventually its doom, when a special effect went awry years later.

The troupe needed a theater, of course, because their livelihood was always at risk, with plague forcing closures and the risk of angering the bureaucrats in the government who looked down on boys playing women's parts and rowdy innuendo-laden plays. Besides, their sometime actor and regular scribe was very much in the favor of the Queen despite his perhaps sometimes Catholic leanings. As long as they had him in town and he wasn't summoned home by Anne, they needed a place to perform the words of William Shakespeare.

Dead Media. Thirty-two-bit color is the typical standard for a computer display these days. Silicon is, of course, sand, and lightning powers all electronics.

The Spencer Wheelhouse. I was in Kannapolis, North Carolina, on vacation. My dad had recently moved there. Naturally we were exploring the area—did you know that they claim Salisbury steak comes from the time a train's chef didn't have a T-Bone for a passenger, so he made him two burger patties mashed together as they pulled into the Salisbury station here?

In fact, the area's history is heavy on the trains. And hence the poem, which resulted from our visit to the North Carolina Transportation Museum. I later arranged this as a song as well.

"The Wreck of the Old 97" was one of the first massively popular sound recordings, and was also the subject of the first major copyright case in the United States.

4-6-0 is a wheel arrangement for trains.

Change of Dreams. The continent of trash is real,[6] by the way—try a Google search for "Trashlantis." *Argosy* was an adventure stories magazine in the pulp days—I grew up reading story reprints from it. I do recall the one about the giant jewfish—apparently the fish is now named something else because the original name might offend. Oh, and Hy Breasil is pronounced "Hy Bree-sal."

The Sargasso Sea is still there, of course. It's just lost its sense of mystery.

The other references I leave to you... they're all easy.

Maid Marian. In between the French tales (which aren't proven to be linked to the Robin Hood Marian, by the way) and her joining the merry men, there's a robust tradition of Marians and Tucks as part of spring festivals, likely as a descendant of earlier Briton practices. Not necessarily as a warrior type, but definitely as a central and key element in terms of fertility/harvest folklore. Marian didn't join the Robin Hood legend until around the 16th c., Robin himself dates to around the 13th c., but Marian figures go back several hundred more years.

As far as Marian being dead—well, this poem was written in response to the second season ending of the BBC's *Robin Hood* TV show, in which they actually killed Maid Marian off, to the great dismay of every viewer. The show didn't last long after that.

Amelia on Nikumaroro. This poem was written in response to the news of investigations by a research group into the possibility that Amelia Earhart's last days were spent on a small atoll called Nikumaroro, also known as Gardner Island.

Itasca was the Coast Guard cutter following her flight across the Pacific and awaiting her at Howland Island, where she was supposed to land. There are

---

[6] http://www.greenpeace.org/international/en/campaigns/oceans/pollution/trash-vortex/

numerous reports of messages from her plane after the crash.

On Visiting Wordsworth. You can read Wordsworth's "Michael" here: http://www.bartleby.com/41/372.html

A Three Kingdoms Story. The poem was written while in Taiwan at a park that has a memorial to Zhuge Liang. It was he who supposedly played the guqin, a zither-like instrument, to avoid an attack on a city.

Jungle Book. These poems were all written based on the level design I did in the Seoni Jungle area of *LegendMUD*. I have never been there; this is entirely based on Kipling's book.

Valley in Ancash. This references the Ancash earthquake[7] that destroyed the village of Yungay. However, it also grew to involve much of my experience of Latin American politics, somehow, catalyzed by a reading I attended by the remarkable poet Carolyn Forché, whose work chronicled much of the political abuses prevalent in the region. And now, it is called to mind both by the events in the Middle East, where the cycle of violence continues, "gross and unmanageable," as inevitable and incontrollable by the common man as earthquakes are; and by an Internet debate on abortion[8])—simply, I think, because of the gaping chasm between worldviews evidenced there, a chasm that is the sort of gap that leads to violence. Or perhaps I think of this because my kids spent a gleeful weekend at Boy Scout camp learning to throw tomahawks, of all things: just the sort of violent useless thing we teach because it seems inborn in us to enjoy the solid thunk of metal into a yielding target.

There is some sense in which it's all just shit the universe throws at us. And we're part of the universe, and vigorously help toss the crap. There is some sense in which the death that comes, well, it comes, regardless of source, and it matters little to those who are dead. "The manner of a death" matters to those who survive; the dead are beyond caring. And the battles fought in the name of the dead to generate more dead... well, everywhere we step is a cemetery, as I

---

[7] https://en.wikipedia.org/wiki/1970_Ancash_earthquake

[8] I stumbled upon the conversation on this site: http://marchtogether.blogspot.com/2006/07/satire.html but it started with a satirical piece, http://www.theonion.com/blogpost/im-totally-psyched-about-this-abortion-10931.

have said before.[9]

I wonder which is the more honest acceptance of our history: to carefully tend the bones in shrines and memorials, granting them the respect and dignity of a life lived and then lost; or to accept that they build the very earth beneath us and are nothing but the by-product of history, meant to be discarded.

By that I don't mean that we should ignore the memories—that's how we keep perpetuating the cycle. But it sure does seem that we fail to learn from them.

On the other hand—the sterility of these actions, the utter fruitlessness of blowing up yet another building, another bus, another village—that's also an illusion. Death is not a sterile thing. Death is a ferment of new life, life we don't expect or want. That boulder I reference in the poem, the one with no leaves, no moss, no nothing but markerhood, probably did harbor life. And every ruin becomes the foundation for a new building. We're repurposers, and our conception of the past as worth preserving is a spotty and recent one; we prefer to build on the middens and graves of our ancestors, victims, and conquerors. From each of these things comes something new—not better, just new. And to be the source—even involuntarily—of this newness is not necessarily a bad destiny. Each person's arc in the sweep of history is tragic: we are born to great hopes, we do our work, strive to perpetuate, and then die without passing on all our learning and without apotheosis. We leave things undone and people behind. But the arc of history—ah, a stumbling drunkard sort of progress, but progress, I think, nonetheless.

And in that sense, being the foundation stone of mountains, being the bricks upon which the future road is built, well, that's no bad thing.

Modus ponens. A meditation on good and evil and faith and logic via *Principia Mathematica*, based on the news that week that some genes for violent antisocial behavior had been identified.

It turns out that up to one percent of the population may have these genes. But they do not always express, because nurture and life circumstances are just as important in whether or not the person's actually going to turn out antisocial, or dare I say it, evil. And yet, we have so often ascribed these behaviors, throughout history, to the Devil, or to other supernatural causes.

I ended up linking this to the notion that religion exists in our mental space in a position analogous to Gödel's incompleteness theorem, which in its

[9] http://www.raphkoster.com/2006/03/19/the-sunday-poem-wandering-near-nazca/

❖ 118 ❖

broadest layman interpretation states that a system cannot prove its own consistency; wasn't there something religious, in the end, in Russell and Whitehead's belief in complete systems, in the ability of logic to put everything into order?

Watching a Play. I was thinking the morning previous about a poem about the difference between a theatrical costume seen up close, and one seen from far away. Then I abandoned the notion as simplistic. That night the verse "and then the way the light hits/their saddened eyes/the lacework lashes" came to me while reading a detective novel. So here it is.

Life Before Light. I wrote this the day we got back from a few days camping in the mountains with the Cub Scouts. It was fairly warm during the day and quite cold at night, particularly since that last night the Santa Ana winds prevented us from having campfires. I played guitar anyway, fingers numb enough to serve as picks.

Wandering the campsite at 3am, unable to sleep, I was struck by the sight of the Milky Way, something our modern world hides from us.

Circadian. One of the things about conferences is that you never get enough sleep. I seem to have inadvertently acquired a mental skill that is nonetheless fascinating to me. I have developed, in the last year, an extremely accurate internal alarm clock.

No matter what time zone I am in, no matter how much or little sleep I have had, when I set the alarm for a given time, I will reliably wake up exactly ten minutes before it goes off. It happened yet again the morning I wrote the poem—despite the loss of an hour for daylight savings time. Right on schedule, I awaken... looked too dark to be the right time—maybe I get that wonderful chance to snuggle back under the covers and drift for a while. But no—my internal clock was right.

I am most upset at being robbed of ten minutes a day of sleep. I *like* sleep. One of my favorite hobbies. The method my dreams have for waking me isn't always pleasant either—that night, it was being a detective in a TV show, and I awoke when I was shot by a suspect and written out.

Anyway, here's the poem, written fresh that morning, still piping hot from the oven. Apologies for the puns, bonus points to anyone who spots them all.

Caledonian Creation Myth. This is called "Caledonian" because that is where I wrote it: at the Caledonian Hotel in Edinburgh.

[citation needed]. This poem is, in part, about the ways in which conflicting points of view make the process of creating Wikipedia rather difficult. NPOV stands for "neutral point of view" in Wikipedia lingo, and "[citation needed]" is what is placed as a footnote next to unverified facts in articles.

The State of Poetry. Posting the Sunday Poem each week became an interesting exercise. For one, few read them. For another, it's something alien enough to the game world that I doubt most regular readers of my blog have any interest. I am sure that the various marketing types who hung out there would tell me that it "dilutes the brand" to some degree, because blogs that are tightly focused (and unambiguous, and full of bullet points!) are the ones that quickly get lots of traffic. Ah, the odd ways in which commerce intrudes.

There are also all the overtones of bad poetry—some of which I have no doubt posted. There's oodles of LiveJournals with atrocious wordsmithing, the sort of thing that once lived safely within the pages of unicorn-speckled notebooks or Goth-clad folders. Certainly, as I comb through the hundreds of poems I have here, finding ones that don't make me cringe is challenging. It can take years to see how bad a given piece of work is, you see. (Although, interestingly, some of the few poems to garner comments here have been the ones that I dashed off the morning that the poem was "due" so to speak, like "Lions in Vegas").

In the end, posting them is essentially an exercise in avoiding what you, the readers, will think about them. As I have been writing poems since, well, as long as I can remember, I have had plenty of cases where the mere offering or existence of a poem was taken the wrong way. Poets fall into such clichéd stereotypes in readers' minds these days: they must be Goth, they must be teenage girls, they must be gay, they must be a pathetic attempt to be romantic…

Diminuendo. Our control over so much of our musical performance is indirect. The subtleties can be great—a slight variation in the pace of a melody, a minor variation in the force with which we tap or pull or blow. In those gaps lies artistry. The difference between bowing one way or another on a violin; a fraction of an inch's difference in how we rest our foot upon the piano's pedal.

Without this, the music lacks humanity. But sound lacks humanity, intrinsically. Sound is oscillation. We are shaping vibrations in the air much like we might plane wood, to give the arched back of a chair a smoother curve. In the end, is it the grain of the wood we admire, or its shaping? Is it the majesty of harmony built into nature, or is it the humanity we see through the gaps in the intervals?

24 Views of Mt. Fuji. This poem is one of several in a series of "painting poems" I did while in graduate school. In these I wrote poems inspired by paintings such as "Girl Before a Mirror," "Nude Descending a Staircase," and others. This one is about the Japanese printmaker Hokusai, whose series of "Views of Mt. Fuji" (there are over a hundred of them) are instantly recognizable to most people. Usually the one people know is the one of the wave.[10] I chose 24 views rather than 36 (the original set) in order to echo the number of hours in a day.

Nude Descending a Staircase. The third of the "painting poems" in this book, it is based on *Nude Descending a Staircase, No. 2,* by Marcel Duchamp.

Guernica. This is a painting by Pablo Picasso depicting the immediate aftermath of the bombing of the village of Guernica during the Spanish Civil War. The painting is a powerful anti-war statement. The poem is about the troubling power of statements in general, regardless of who they are from. All the "painting poems" were about naming, and the power of names to frame things.

Paradise Shark. "Paradise shark" is an alternate name for the common aquarium catfish usually known as the rainbow shark. We've had several of these over the years, though we don't have one right now. The main characteristics of this fish are that they are kind of territorial, chasing away other fish, very much proud of being a "shark"—and that they are only a couple of inches long. They also have little black barbels that look like a cartoon French mustache.

Soul Food. I wrote this after reading a wonderful Connie Willis short story called "Even the Queen," which featured "floratarians," akin to vegetarians but subsisting on flowers alone. It sounded like the kind of thing that would trigger

---

[10] https://en.wikipedia.org/wiki/The_Great_Wave_off_Kanagawa

a diet fad amongst the extremely fashionable.

Goety. I had just finished reading a rather entertaining book, and it reminded me of a word I had not heard in some time: goety. No doubt now I will have dozens of links from weird occult websites, wondering what spells I am about to write out. Or else sites from the holier side, adjuring me.

The fascinating thing to me, of course, is that so many things we see as different had the same root—the basics of mathematics, the principle of zero or the concept of bases, somehow becoming a root of alchemy and numerology. The very fact of writing became prosthetic memory and thence the fruit of the tree of knowledge. The ghosts and demons of the misunderstood world became elaborate and frankly silly rituals that led to the deaths of thousands. The act that we do everywhere around the world, of blogging, the child of a mysterious art that once was deemed powerful and dangerous.

The Pangrammatic Fox. "I've got an even harder challenge than what I suggested previously. Construct a poem, or perhaps a haiku, using only pangrams. That's not the challenge though. The challenge is do that and make sense. I bet you US$1.00 that you cannot do this. It's impossible for even a Master Poet. ;P"–Morgan Ramsay.

For those who do not know, a pangram is a sentence that contains every letter in the alphabet. (A perfect pangram doesn't even repeat any). I went with a pangram per line, and in the spirit of self-enumerating pangrams, made the poem about pangrams, and their most famous exponent.

Some annotations:

• The Zipf distribution is the distribution of words in languages. As it happens, the distribution of letters in the English language follows a similar enough curve that I thought I'd fudge it here.

• Glyphs are, of course, letters.

• Catalexis is when you leave a metric foot off of a line of metric verse.

• Zeugma is hard to explain, but basically it is when you use one verb or noun on two or more clauses of a sentence.

• To coffle is to chain up in a line. "Waxing jabber" can be read quite literally as "increasing talkytalk." So, "numbers chaining up and confining increasing verbiage."

• Reynard is of course the medieval European trickster fox.

• The sieve I am referencing is "sieve theory," not the cooking implement, though really, same difference.

Which brings me to how I wrote it. The answer is, with a little help. I wrote a quickie little program to scan sentences for me and tell me what letters were missing.

Flicker. It's hard to understand, these days, how prized writing once was. Everywhere we turn there is verbal diarrhea, an endless stream of twittering: there's blog diaries and fan fiction and political ideologues, there's spin and truthiness and position papers, there's stories that perhaps don't deserve to be told. We live in a world that is abundant in writing, abundant in books, with little sense of how once each carefully formed letter was a bulwark against the collapse of civilization.

For those of us who are readers, it can be hard to even comprehend. Once upon a time, people went blind for the sake of reading. They copied huge tomes by hand. They knew themselves to be special, people who had access to the magic of accumulated knowledge, an access most did not have. In some times, the material in the books they tended was literally a brick in a wall against barbarism; today we pulp excess books and strain the ink out to make room for yet more words, words, words words.

The Age of the Computer Poem. Back in 2006, Apple encoded a pretty bad limerick in its operating system OSX, to dissuade hackers. It read:

Your karma check for today:

There once was a user that whined
his existing OS was so blind
he'd do better to pirate
an OS that ran great
but found his hardware declined.

Please don't steal Mac OS!
Really, that's way uncool.

I have no idea why they thought that "pirate" and "great" rhymed.

Network Optimization. TCP is a network protocol that underlies much of the Internet. Information sent across computer networks is divided into discrete packets. As they arrive, they are put into memory buffers for temporary storage, which sometimes can overflow and cause issues. K is short for kilobyte, a quantity of computer memory. The header is the part at the top of the packet, sort of like the address on the outside of an envelope. The ack is the message sent back to acknowledge receipt of the packet. MD5 is a hash—basically a special code built out of the content, that you can use to verify that the content arrived correctly.

Both linked lists and maps are common forms of organizing data in a computer program.

Pixels are the dots that make up a graphical image on a screen. Infoviz is shorthand for information visualization, the way in which we display graphs to read what is going on in a complex system. Python is a computer programming language, often used for writing little utilities, such as one that examines why you might be having network issues. It does this by examining the log files— "tail" being a way to look at the end of a file in the Unix operating system. A nybble is half a byte of memory.

I wrote this as I was doing some network code debugging at work one day.

Ode to Code: A Geek Poem. OK, this is for the geeks among us. In fact, it is geeky on many different levels. It merits explanation in advance.

One night, I was working on a game I've been messing with. It's circular, so there's a lot of Sin(a) and Cos(a) and incrementing arcs and stuff. I was up until 4am, in fact, and needless to say, when you do that you end up with dreams. Mix into this the fact that at the Cub Scouts that past week, the demo was of optics, and we saw white light broken into the spectrum, and the wavelengths of the colors identified (and blue is damn close to 440 nanometers, and the note A is of course at 440 as well), an article I read a year before about how the vibration frequency of the universe is the note A, how the composer Schumann (who went insane because of syphilis and mercury poisoning) was driven mad by hearing the note A… well, soon you end up with a poem that mooshes it all together.

Then, to top it all off, I wrote it in blank verse: iambic pentameter, with seven-line stanzas, and one extra coda line (alas, not 440 syllables—290). The stanzas arose organically, but each verse really hated being in lines—words broken across lines, etc., like strands that shouldn't be interrupted. So then I re-broke the lines to be in a sine wave. Because I could. They seemed to want to fall that way. Eerie, huh? So finally, you're left with a poem about, well, making games.

The BASICs of Life. BASIC is an obsolete computer language that was popular in the 1970s and 1980s (there are still dialects of BASIC in use, but they don't much resemble the original anymore!). In BASIC, you needed to start every line with a number. The first word of every line in this poem is actually a command in BASIC; DIM for reserving memory, REM to remark, PRINT, GOTO, FOR and NEXT to do something a set number of times, DATA, WHILE, POKE, and END. POKE was a command that let you alter an address in memory.

If You... Borges' big library is discussed in his short story "The Library of Babel."

About the Author

Raph Koster was born in 1971, has lived in four countries and over a half-dozen different states, and is married with two kids. He holds a bachelor's degree from Washington College in English/creative writing and in Spanish, and a Master of Fine Arts degree in poetry from the University of Alabama. While in college, he also spent time studying most everything in the humanities, including music theory and composition and studio art. He is a past member of the famed Turkey City science fiction writing workshop. His music has been featured on television, and he has released one album, *After the Flood.*

Raph is a veteran game designer who has been professionally credited in almost every area of the game industry. He's been the lead designer and director of massive titles such as *Ultima Online* and *Star Wars Galaxies*; a venture-backed entrepreneur heading his own studio; and he's contributed design work, writing, art, soundtrack music, and programming to many more titles ranging from Facebook games to single-player games for handheld consoles. His book *A Theory of Fun for Game Design* is one of the undisputed classics in the games field. In 2012, he was named an Online Game Legend at the Game Developers Conference Online. This award recognizes the career and achievements of one particular creator who has made an indelible impact on the craft of online game development.

Visit his website at **http://www.raphkoster.com** or follow him on Twitter at **@raphkoster.**

www.ingramcontent.com/pod-product-compliance
Lightning Source LLC
Chambersburg PA
CBHW021506090426
42739CB00007B/495